SCRIBBLE PORTRAITS

Zafaro

DEDICATION

This art book is dedicated to no one.

INTRODUCTION

The art book contains fifty
unique portraits done in scribble art style.

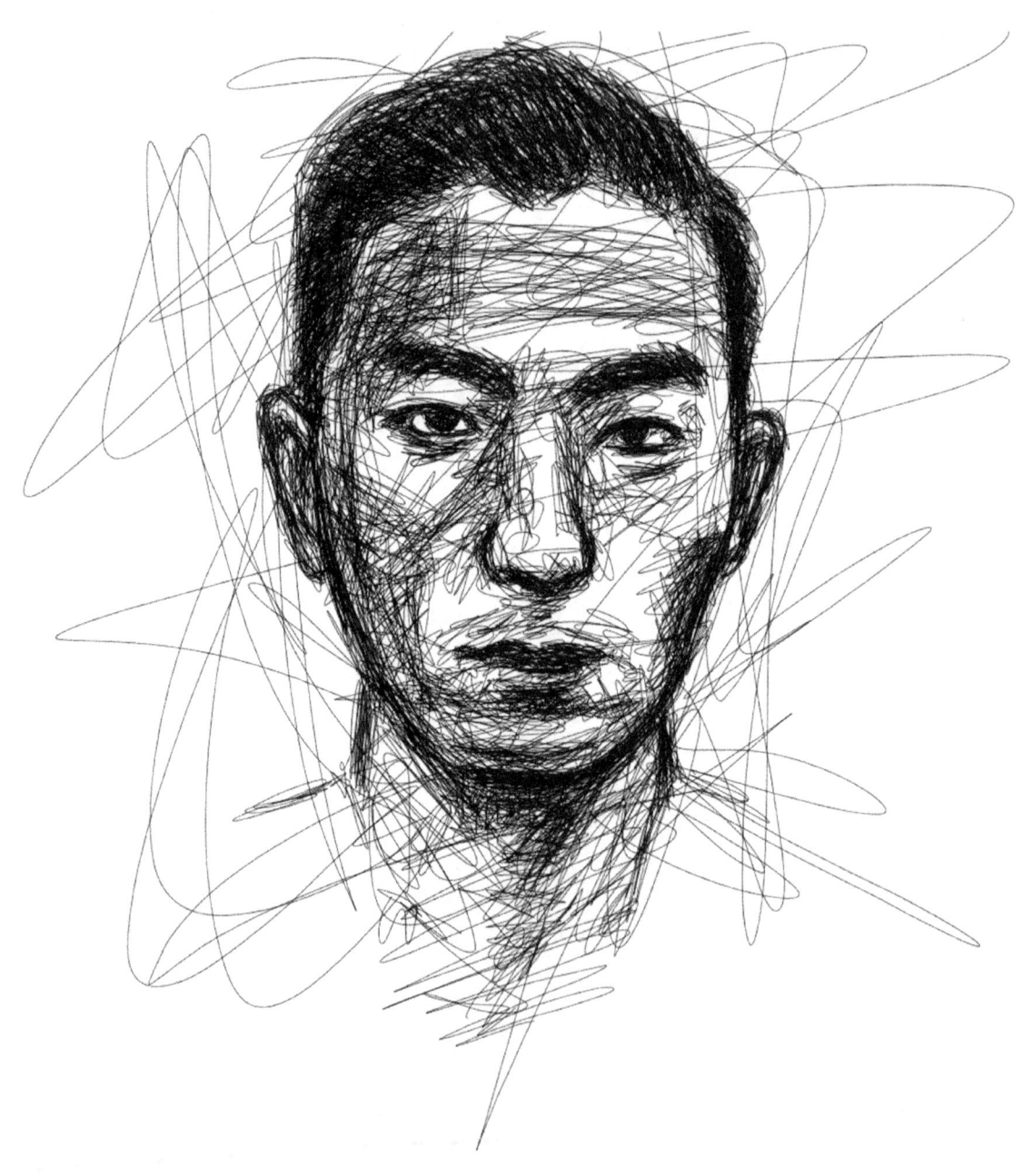

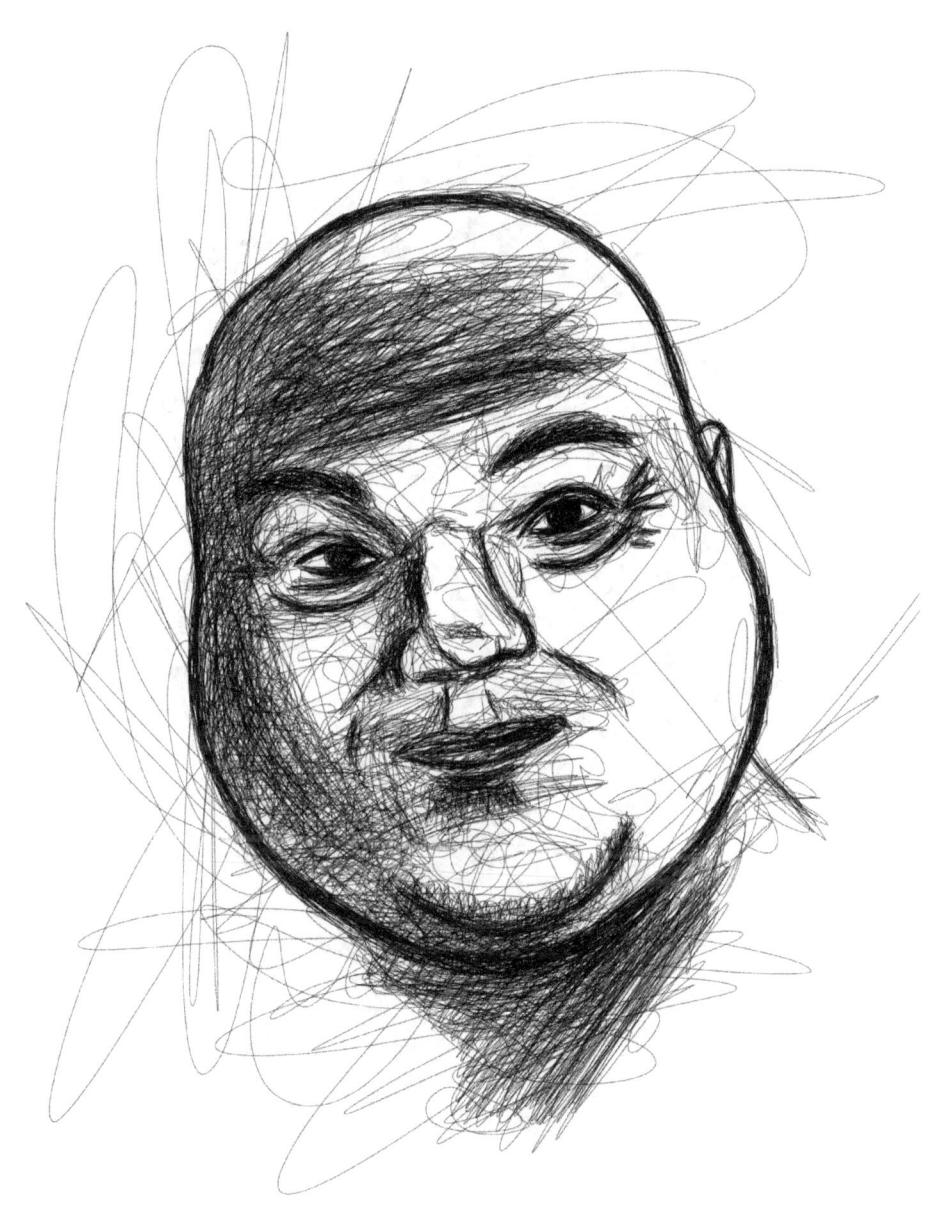

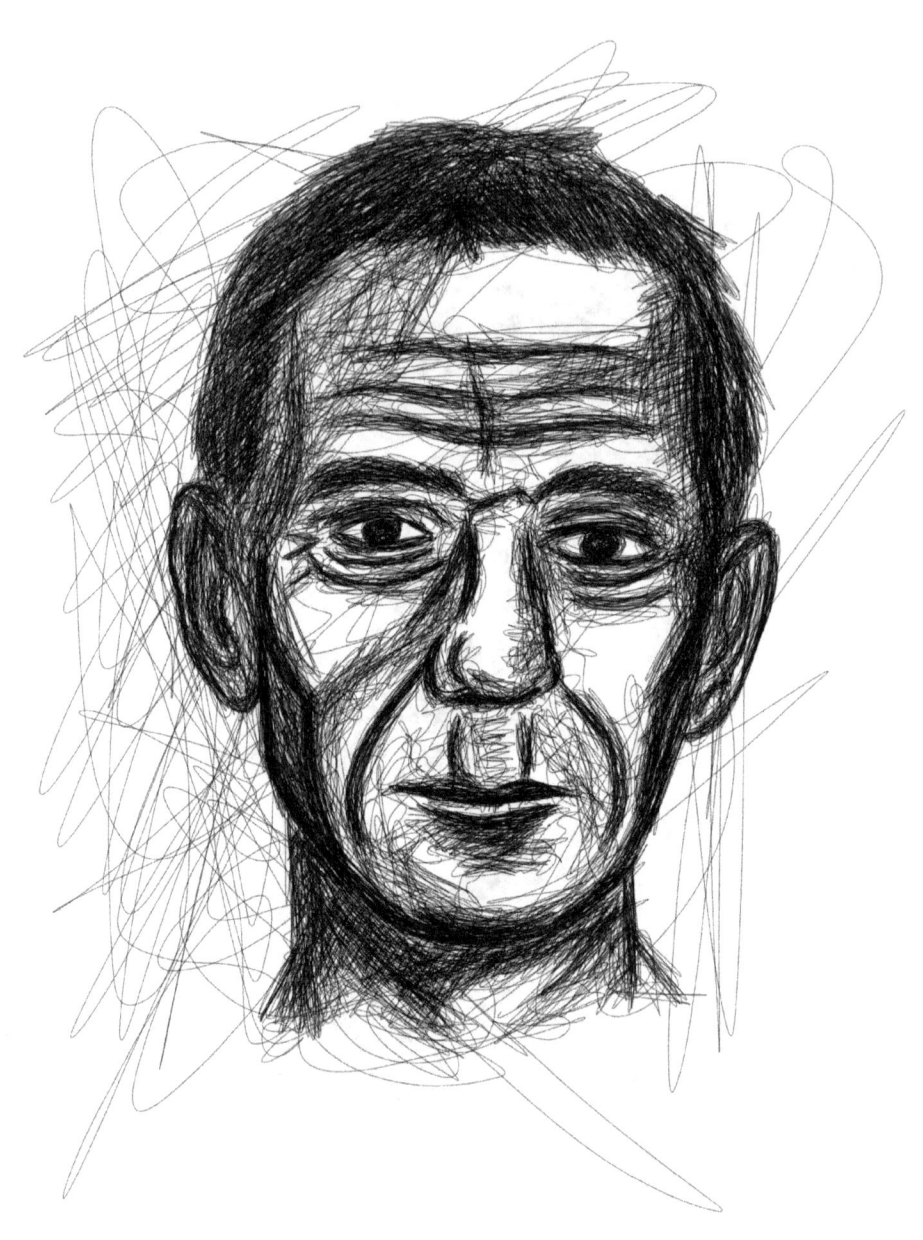

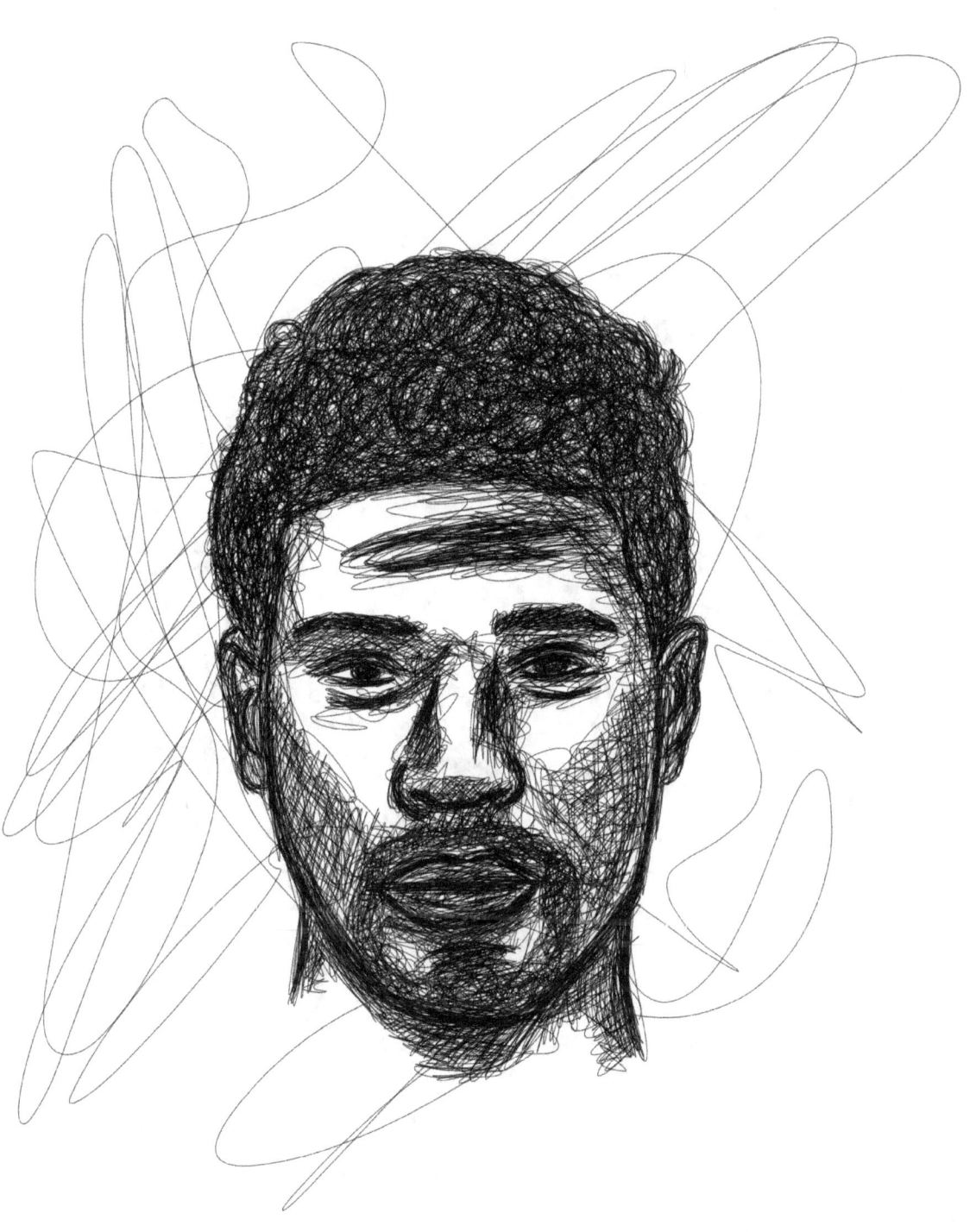

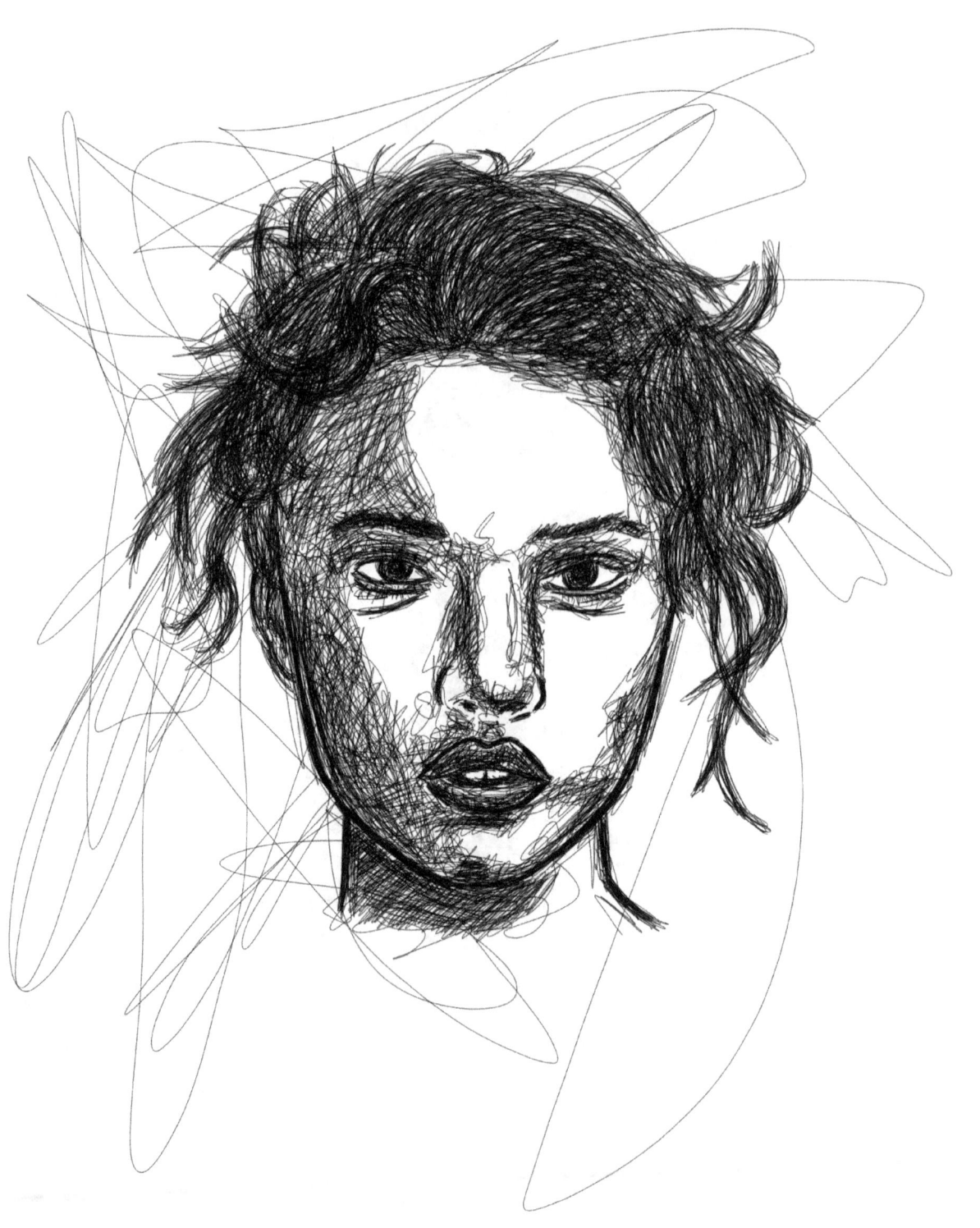

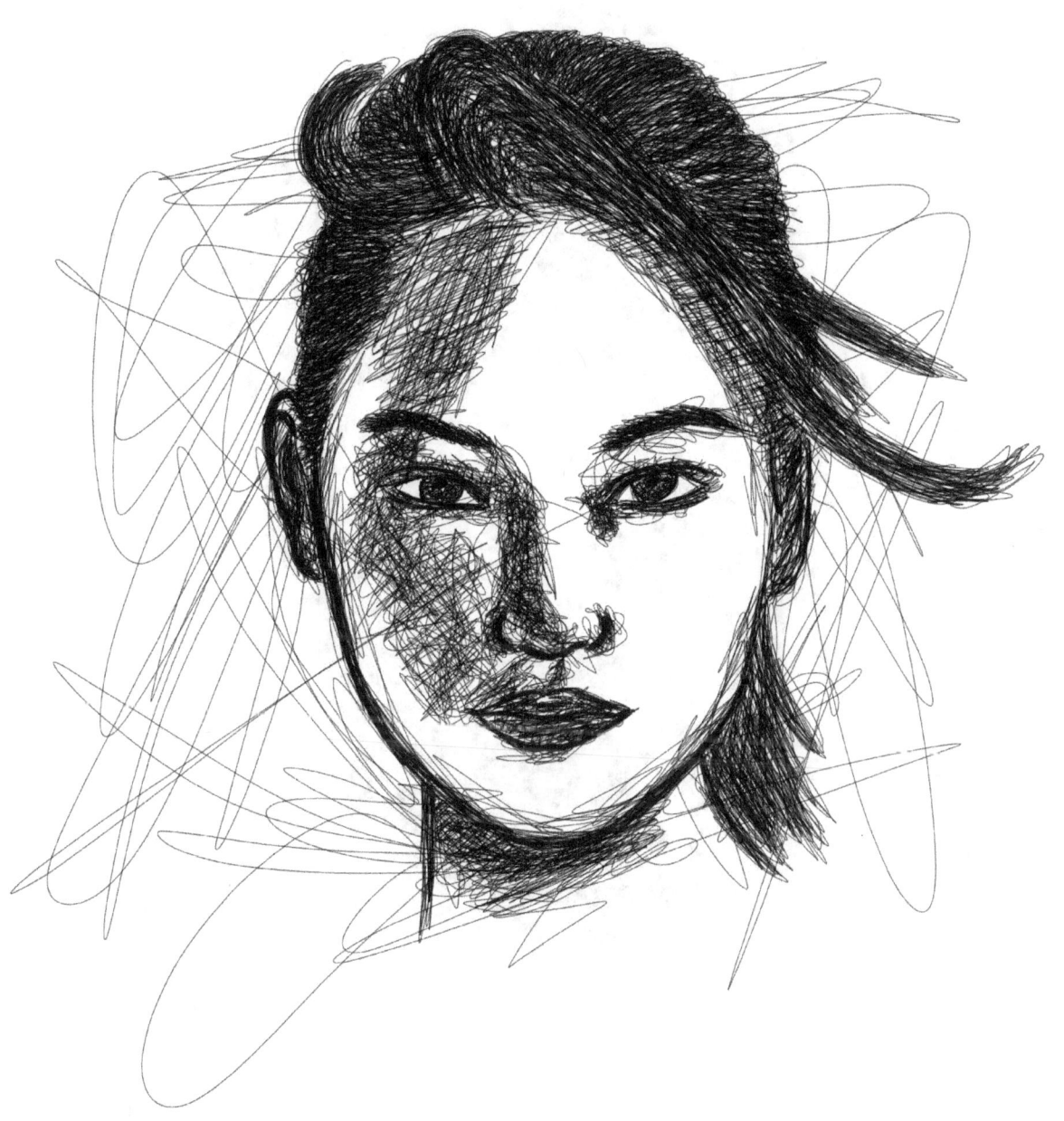

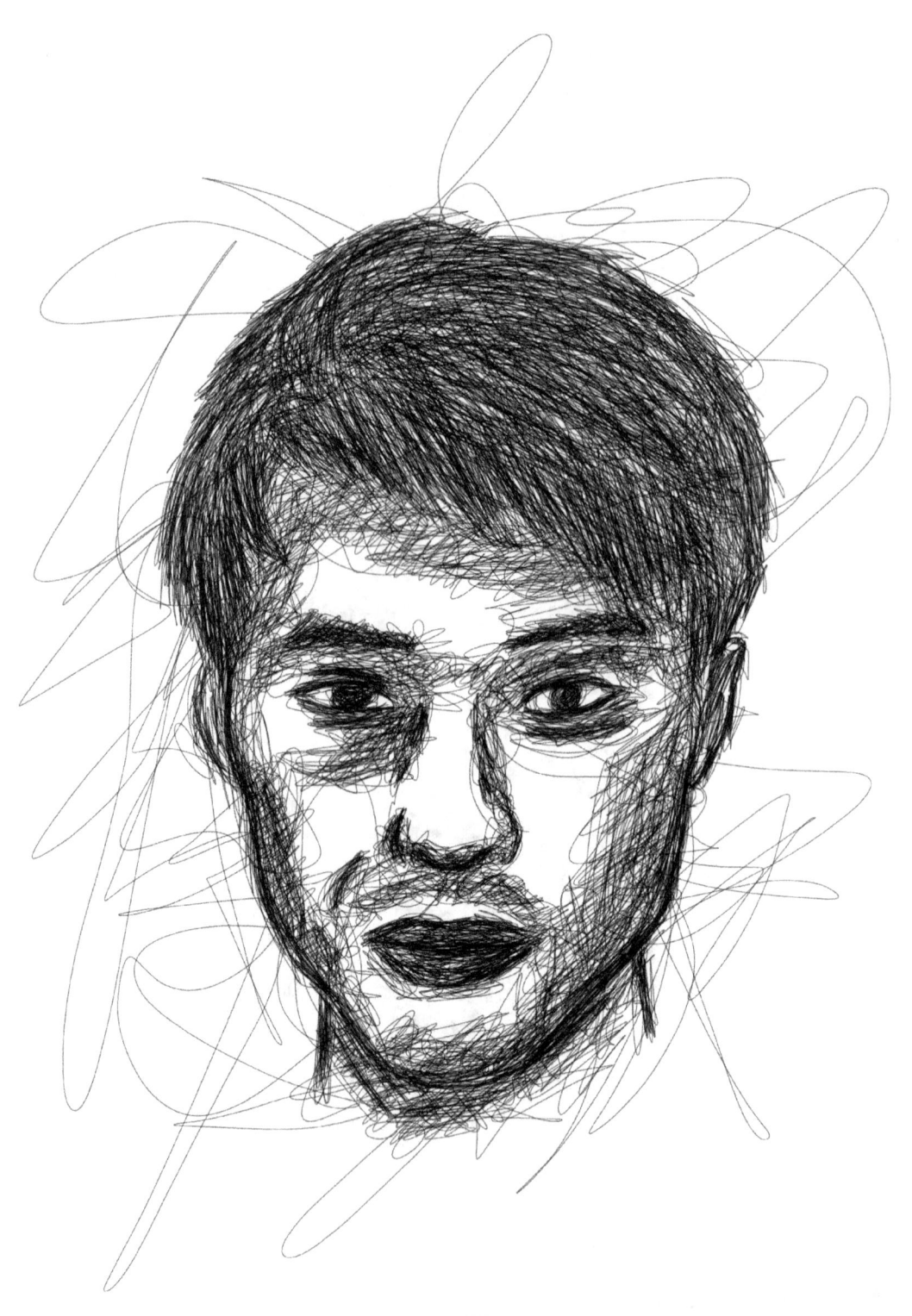

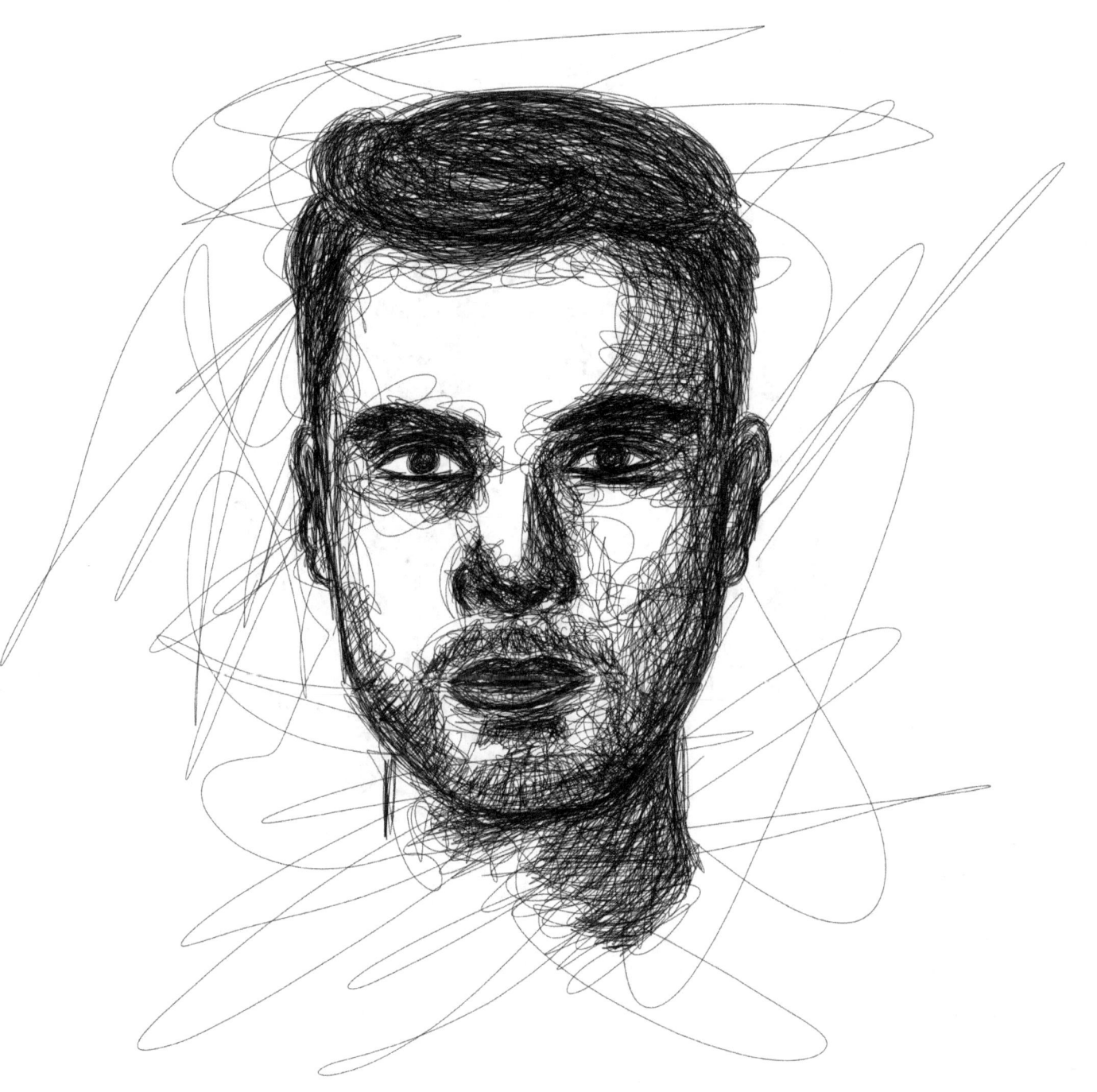

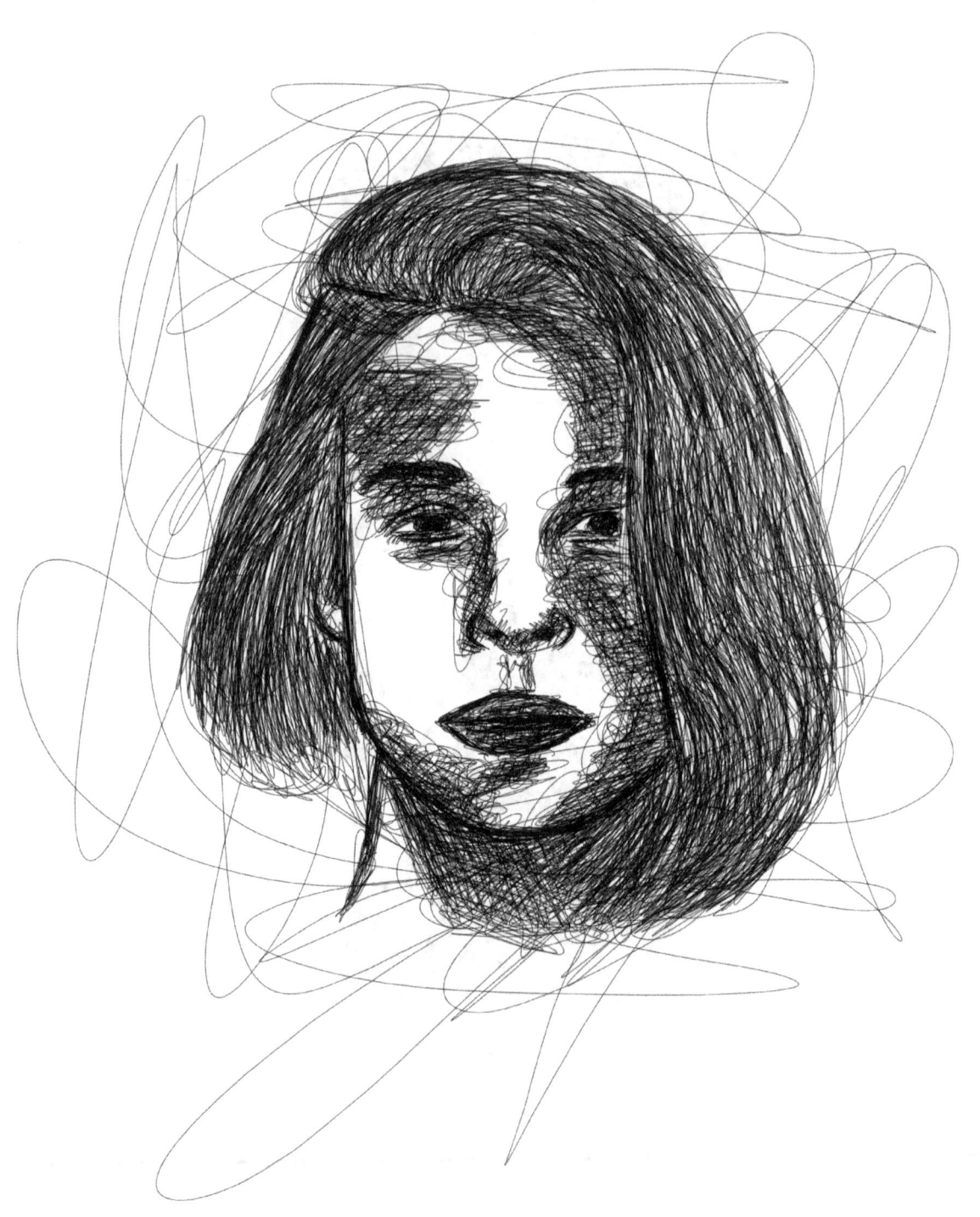

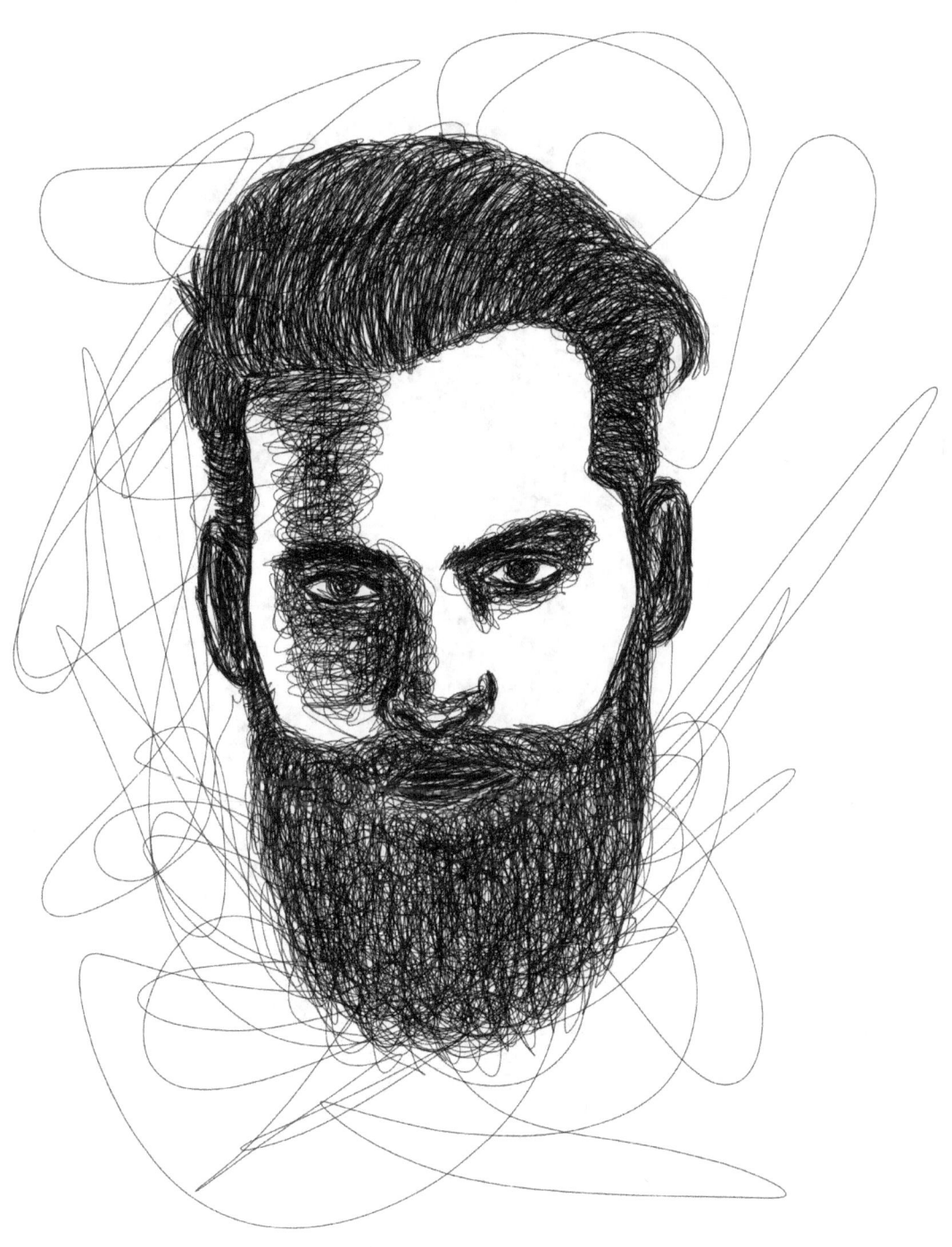

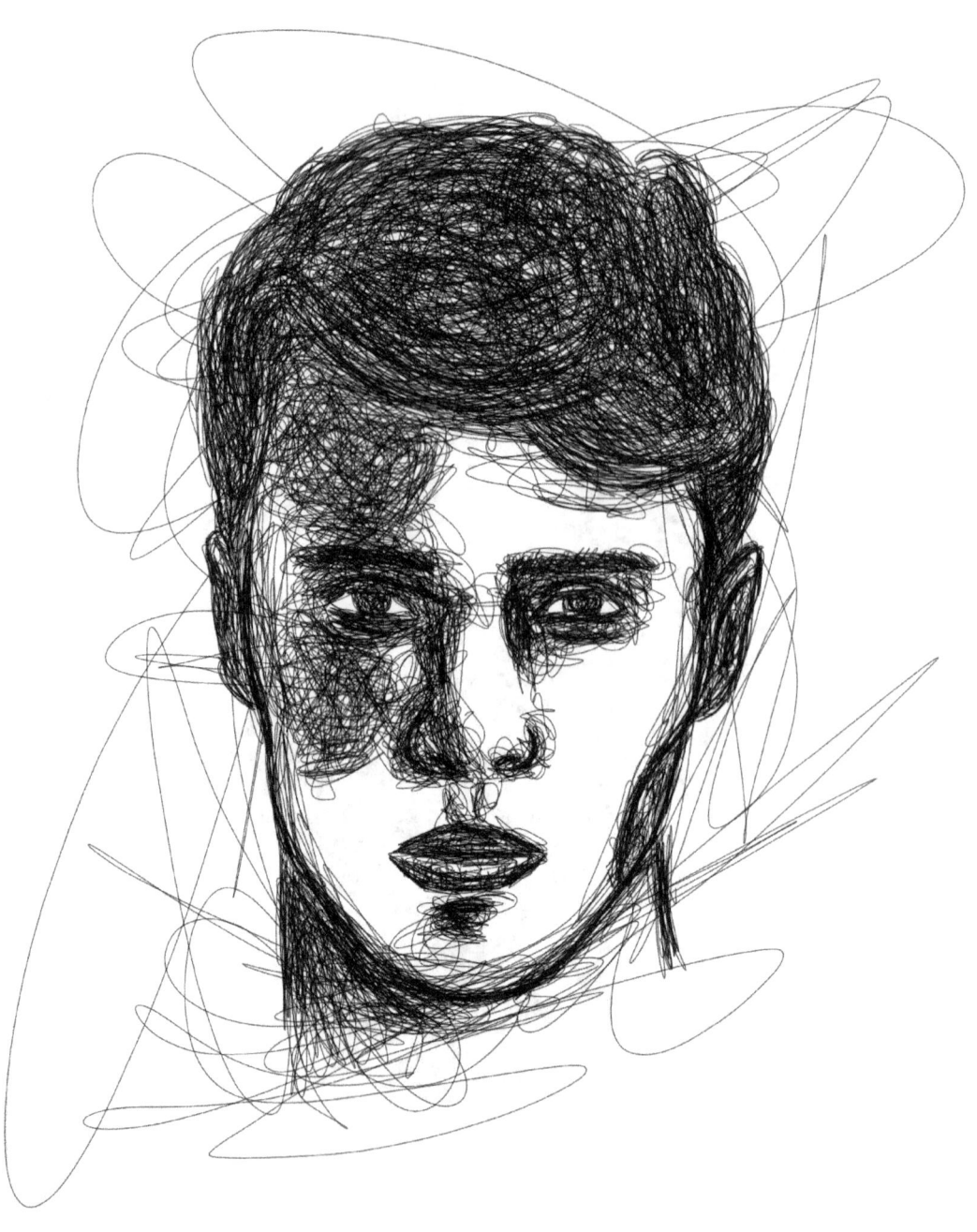

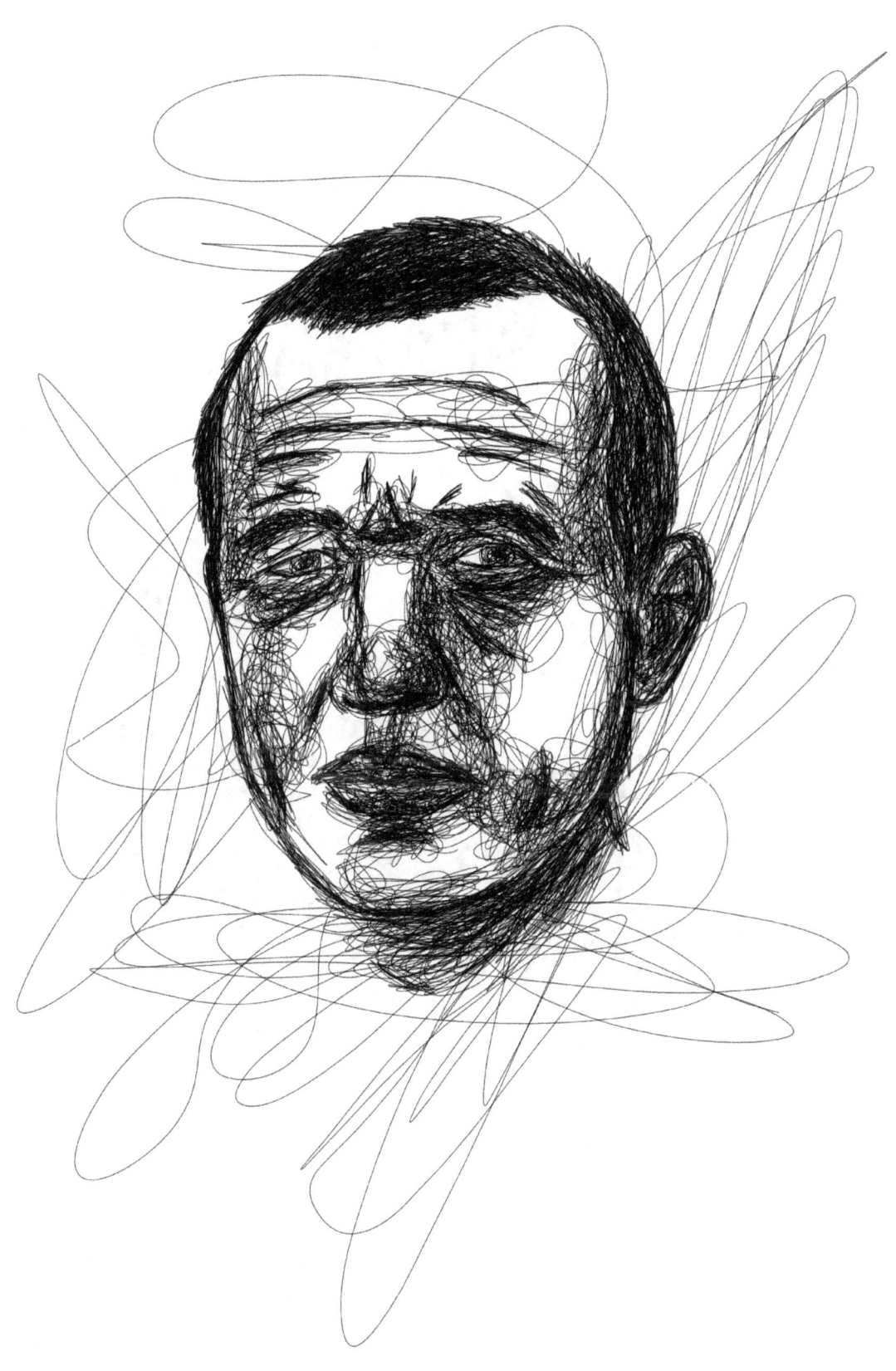

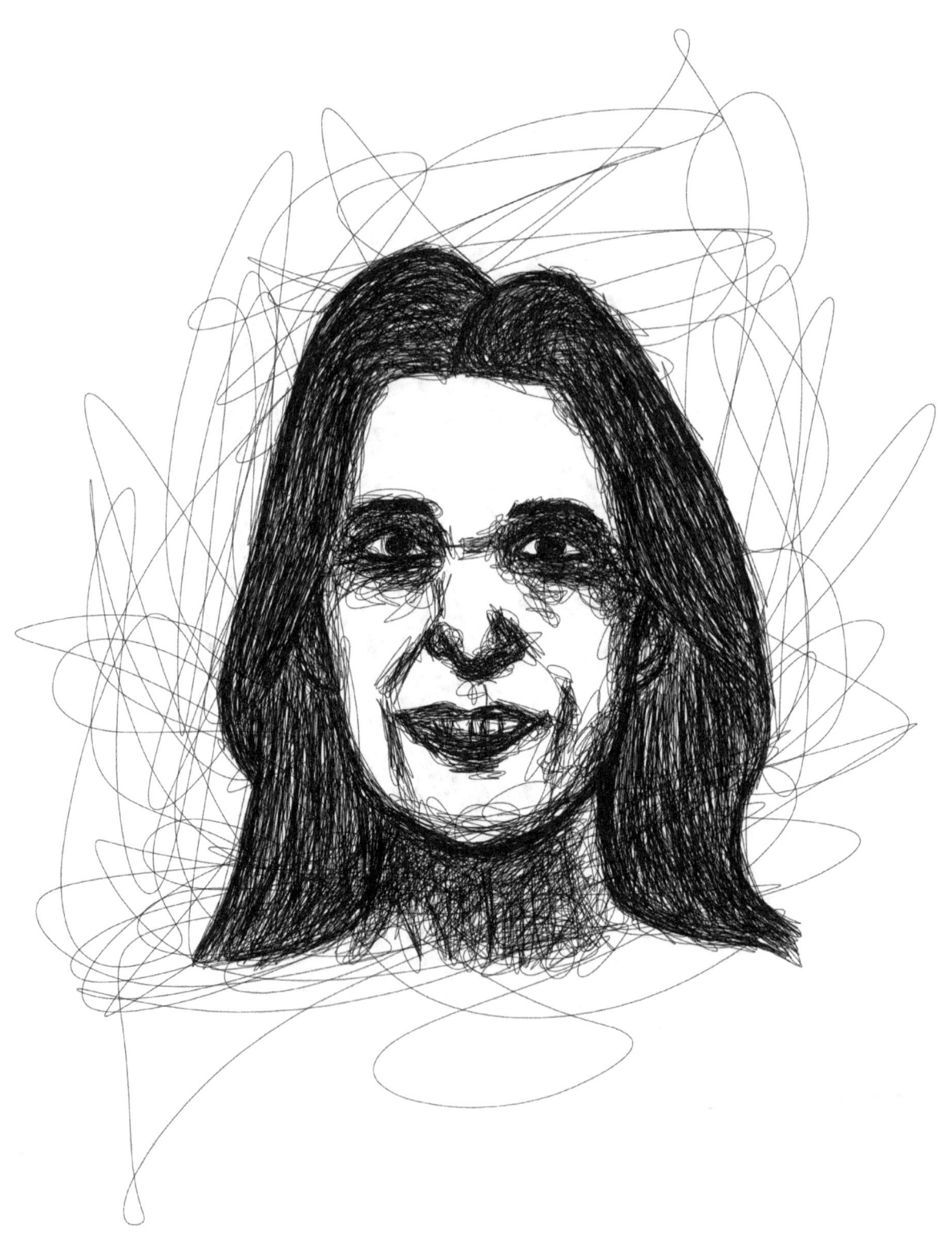

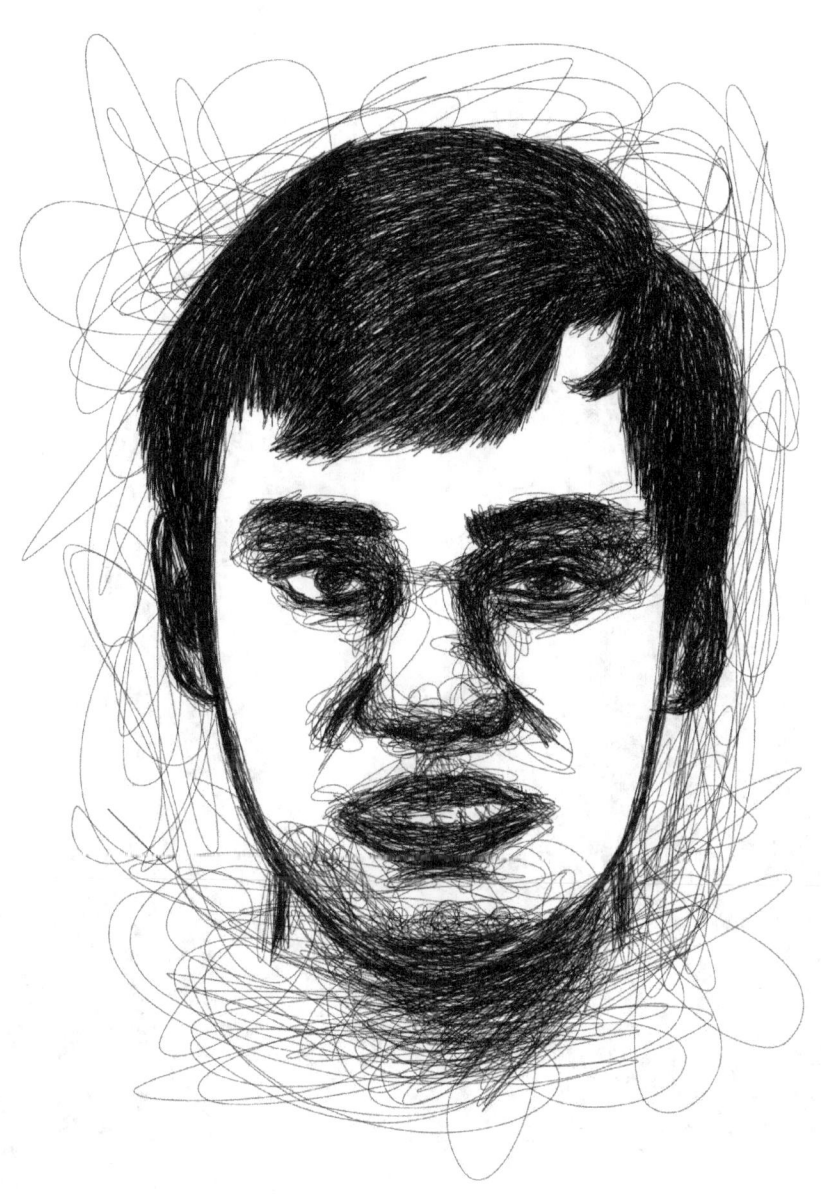

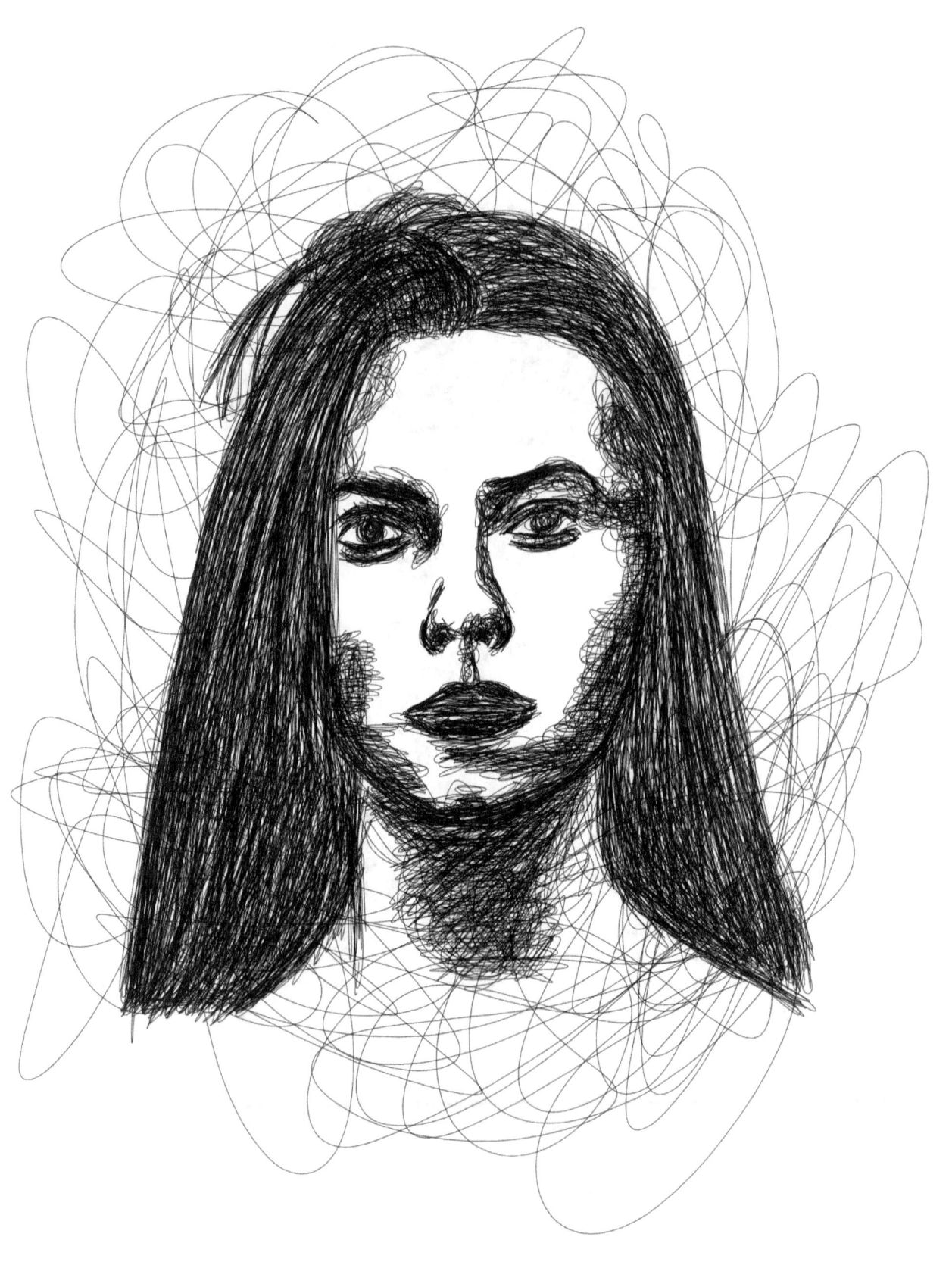

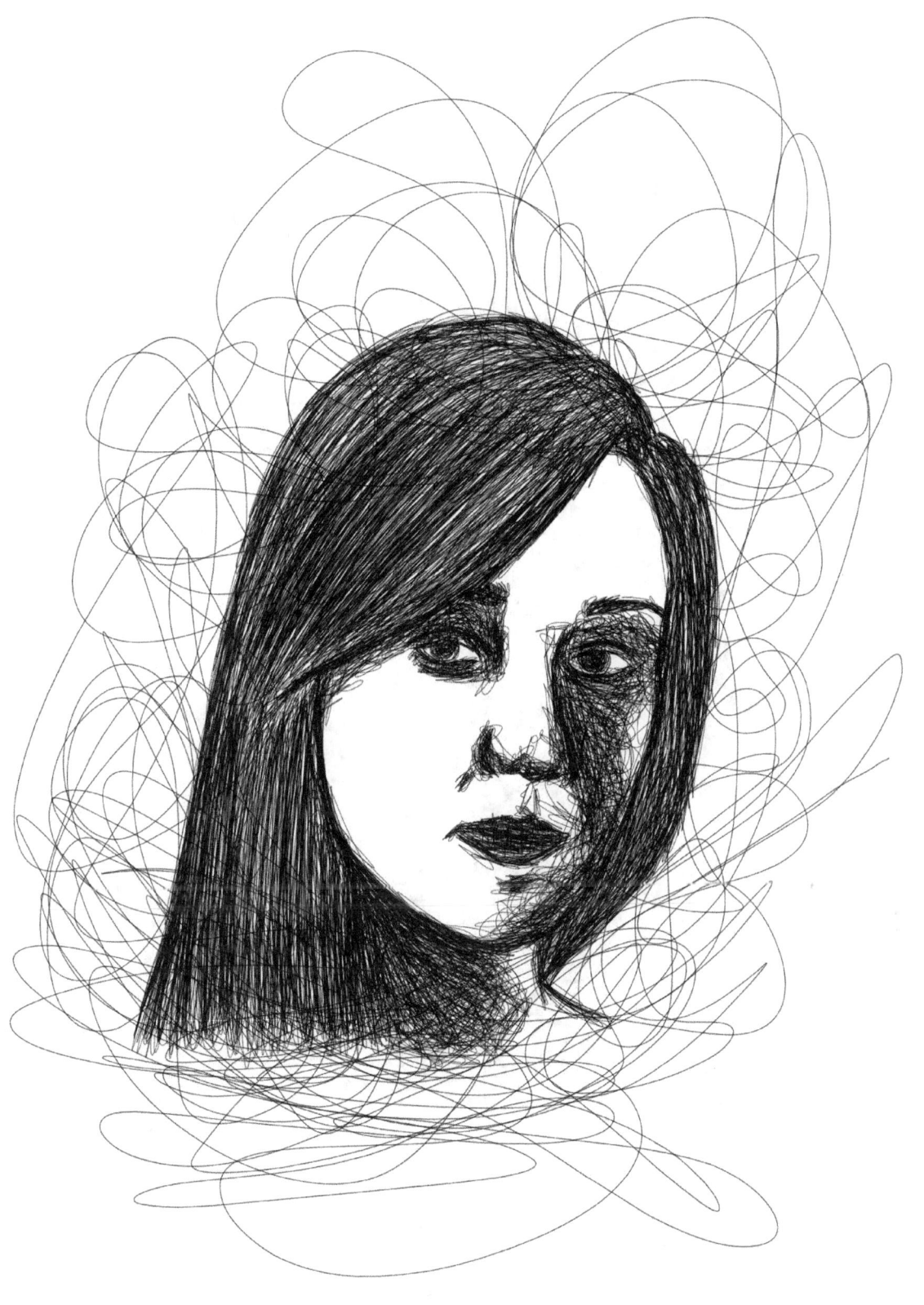

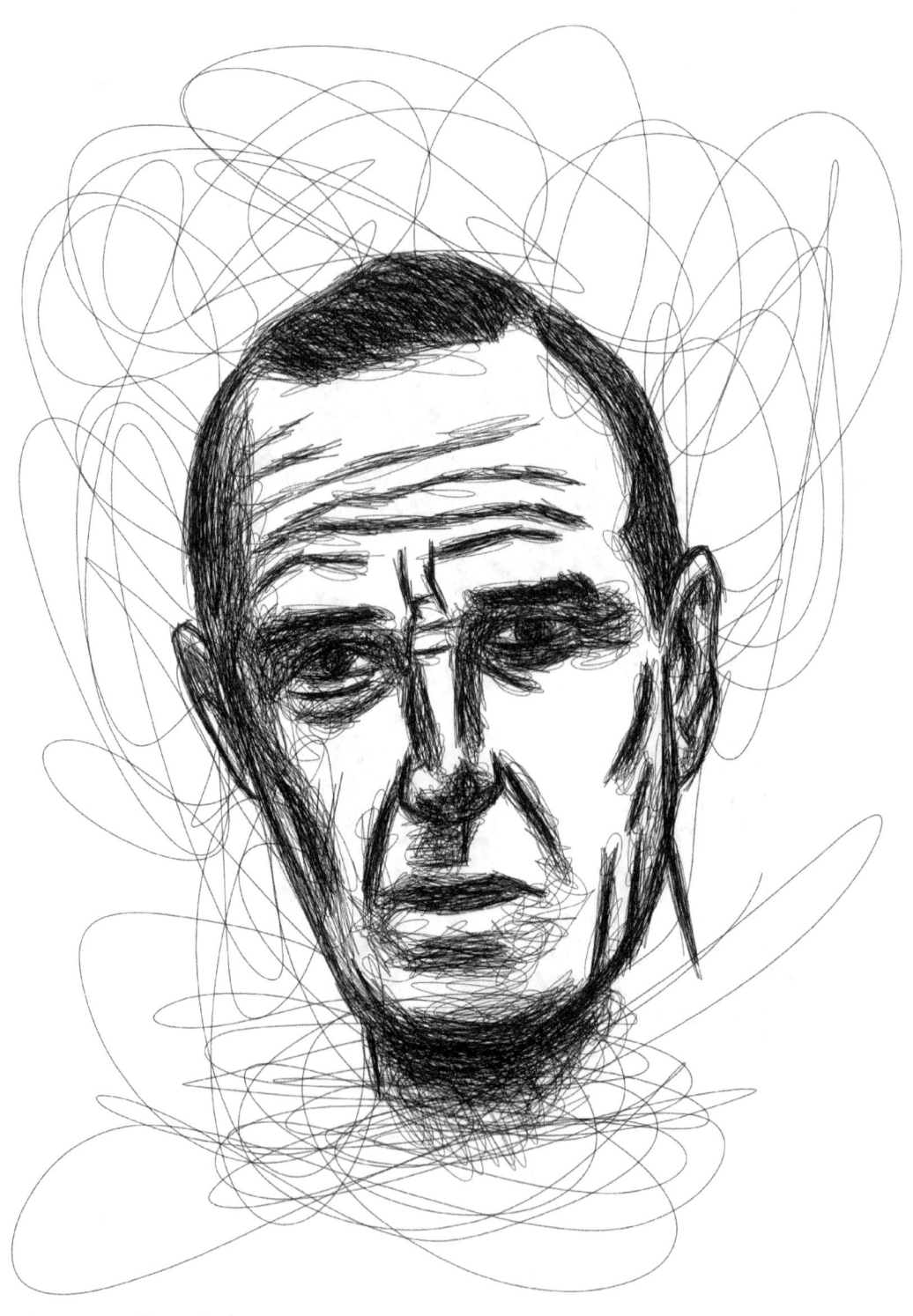

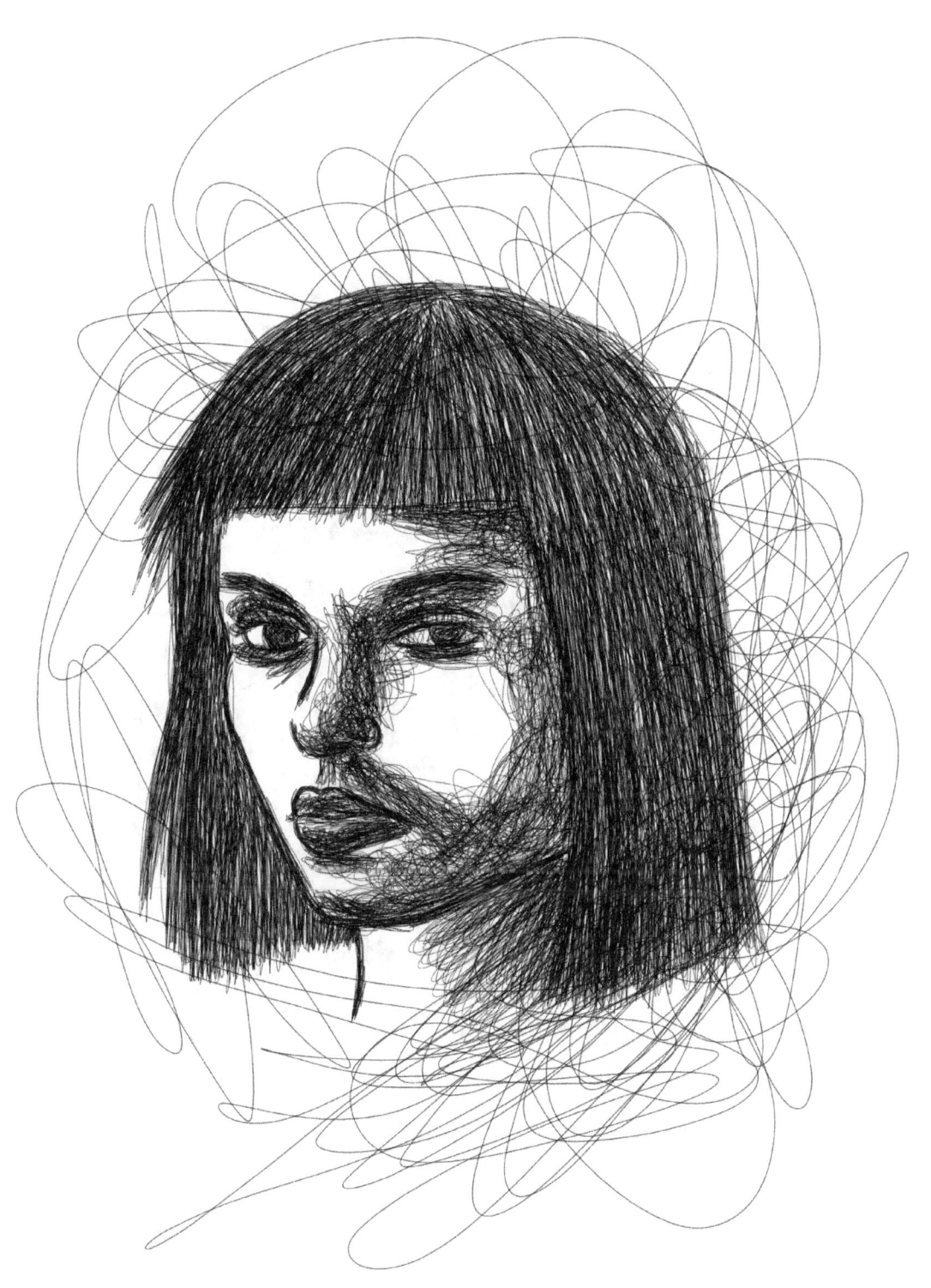

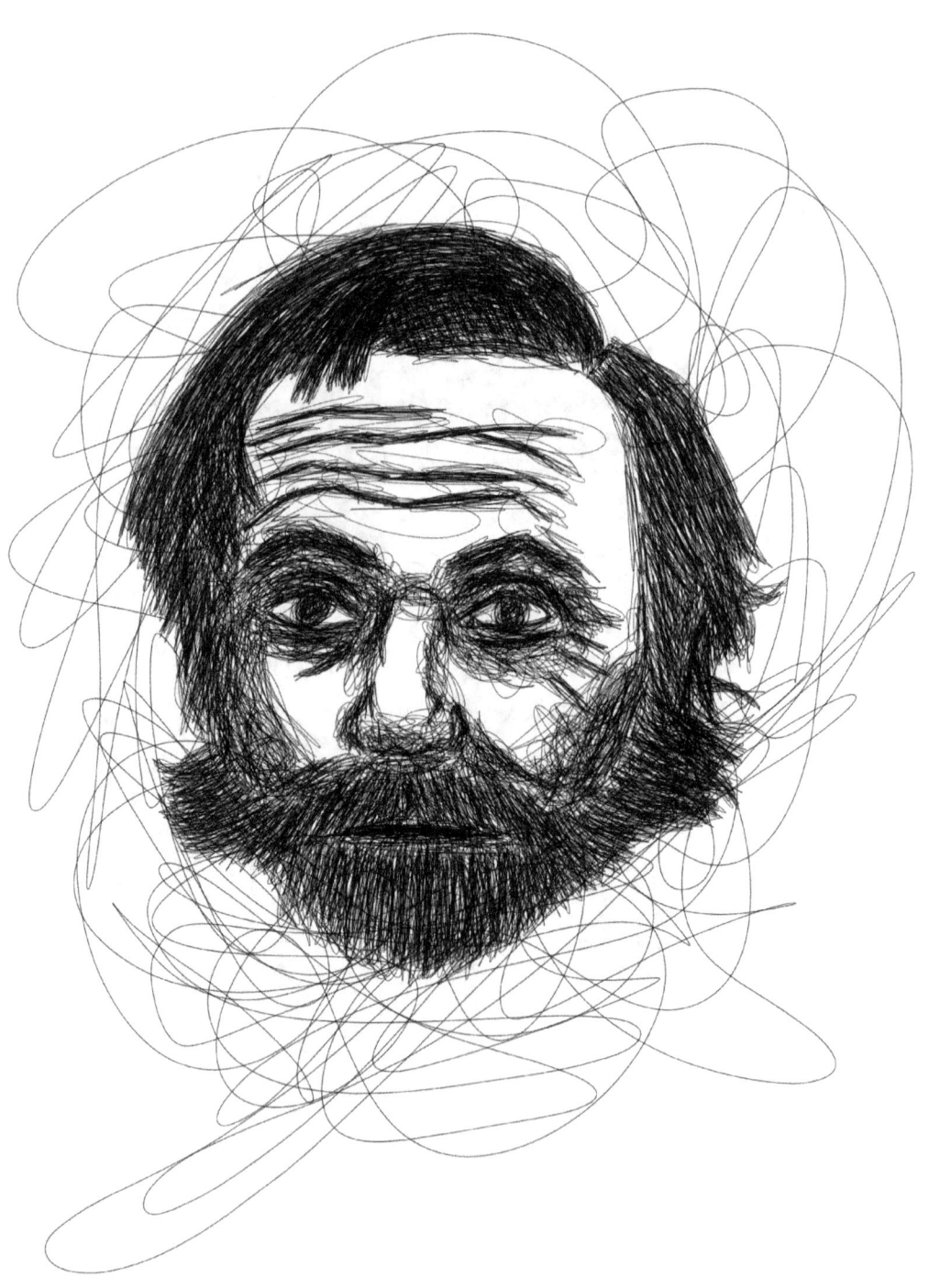

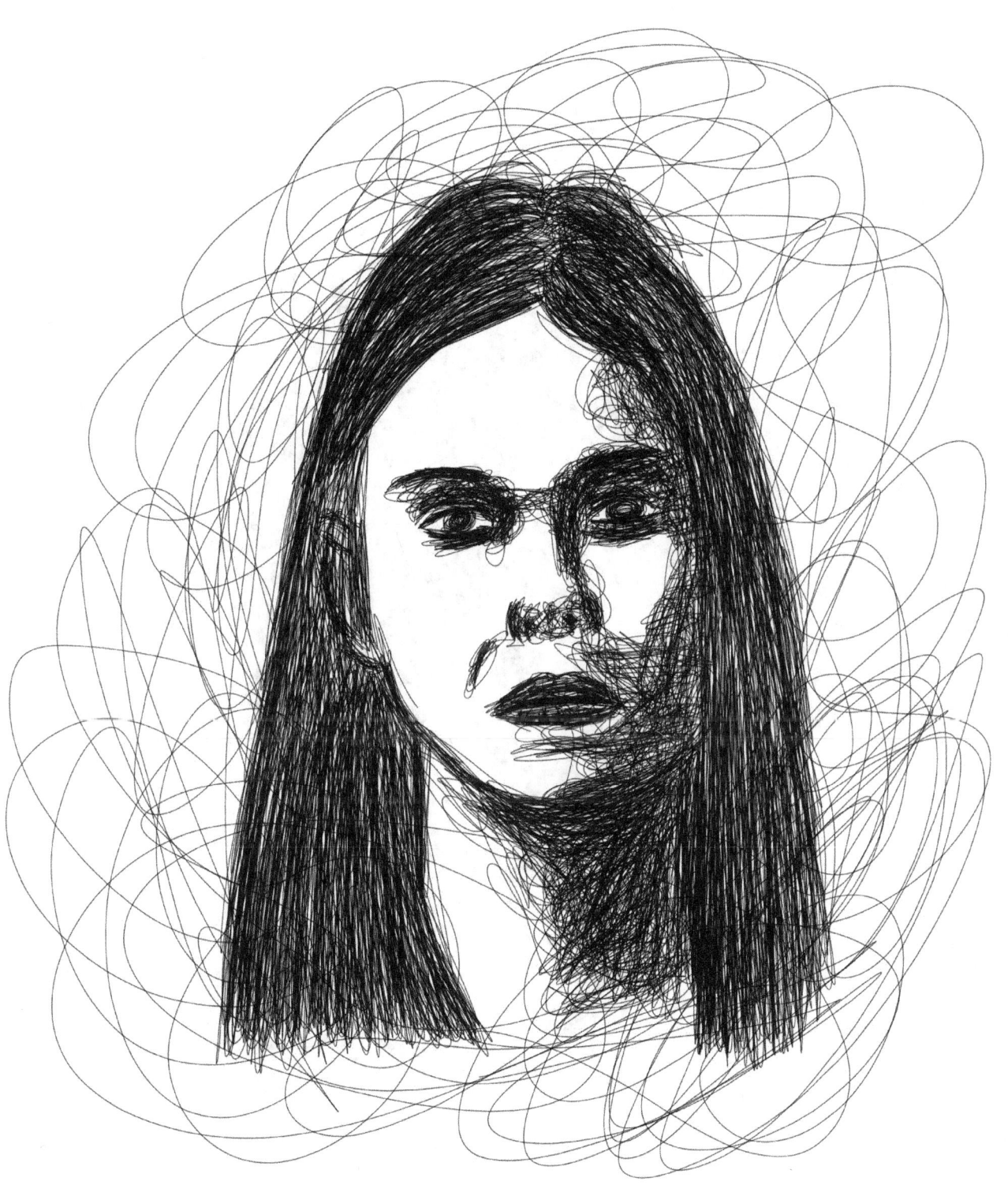

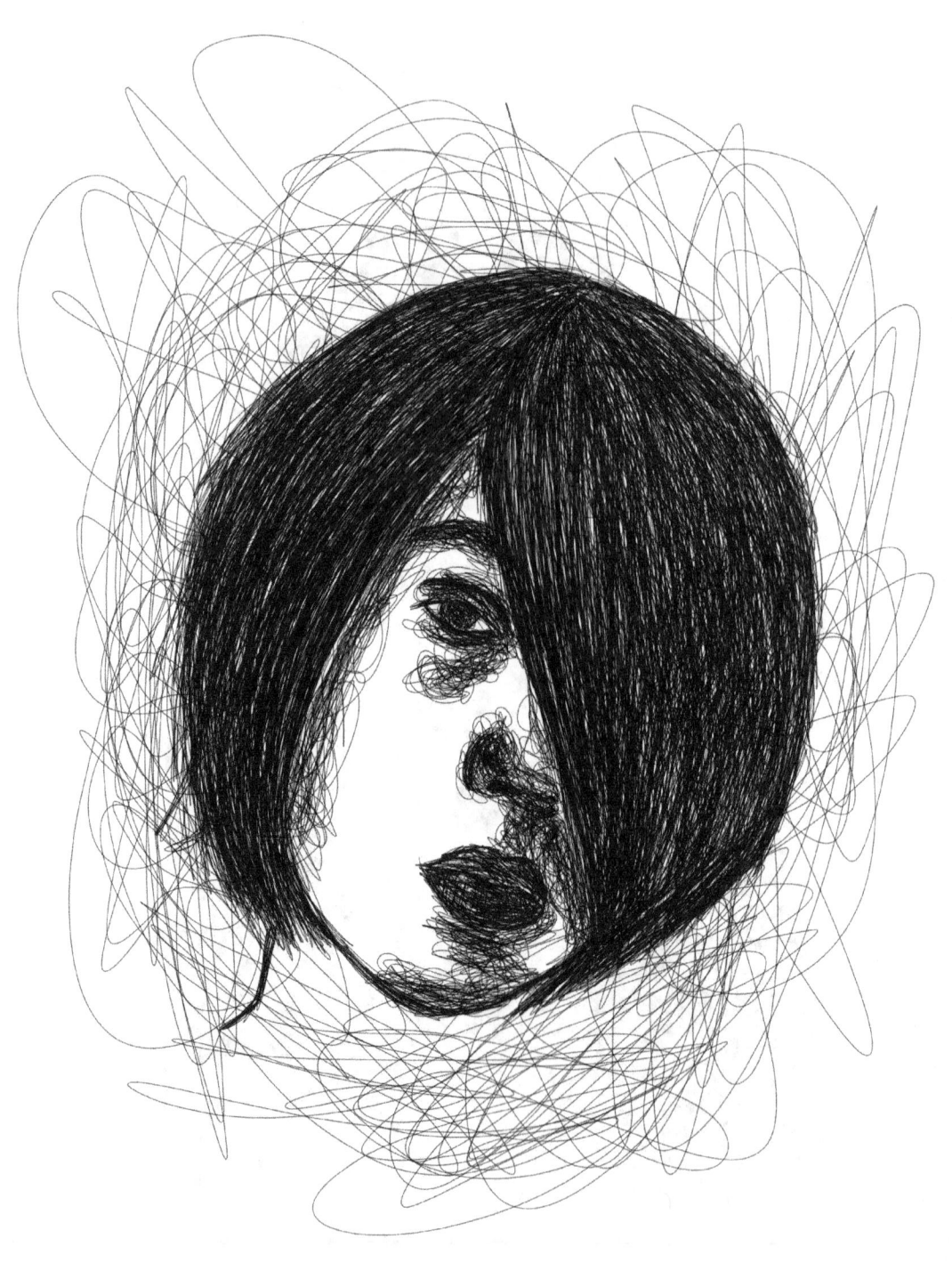

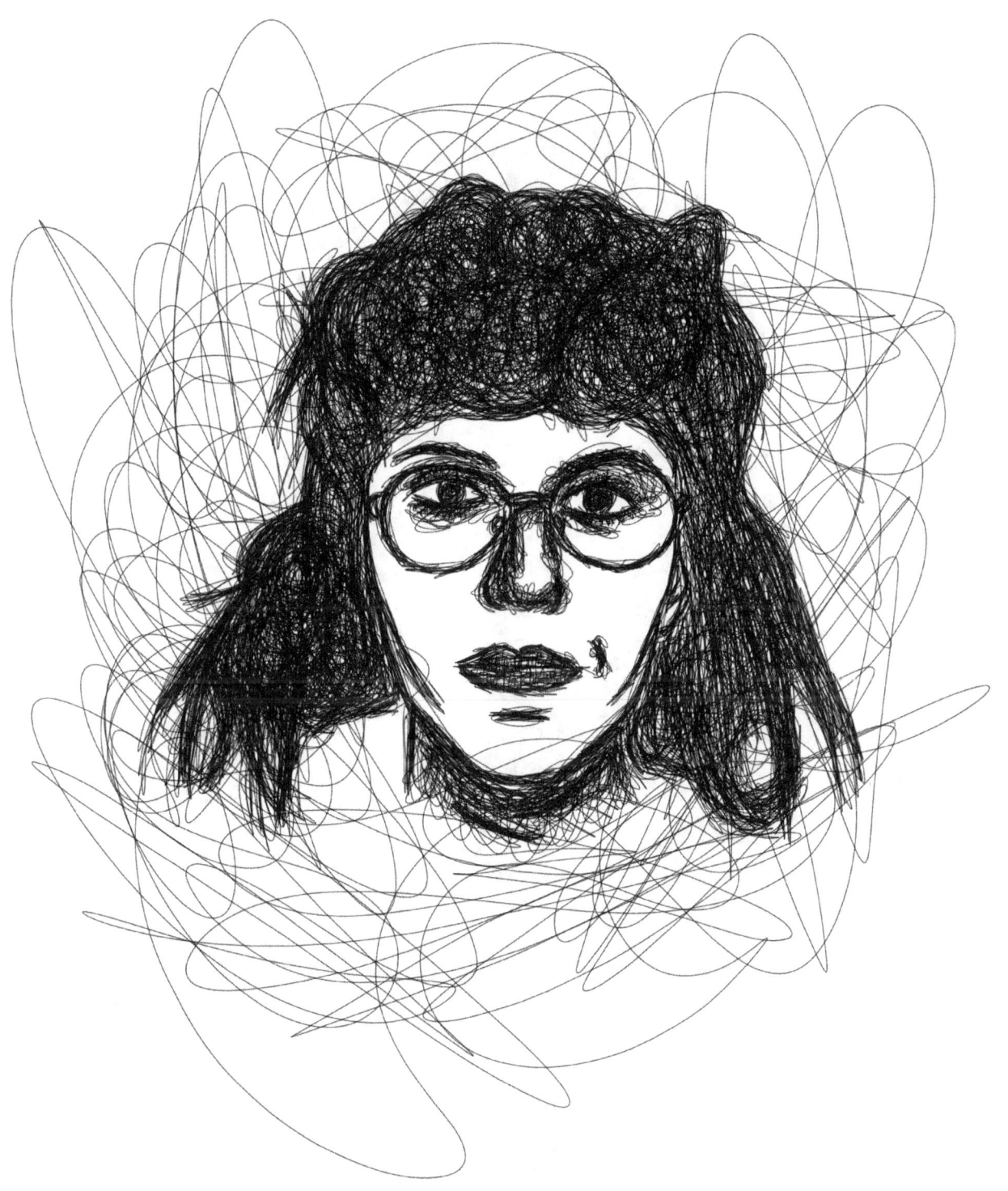

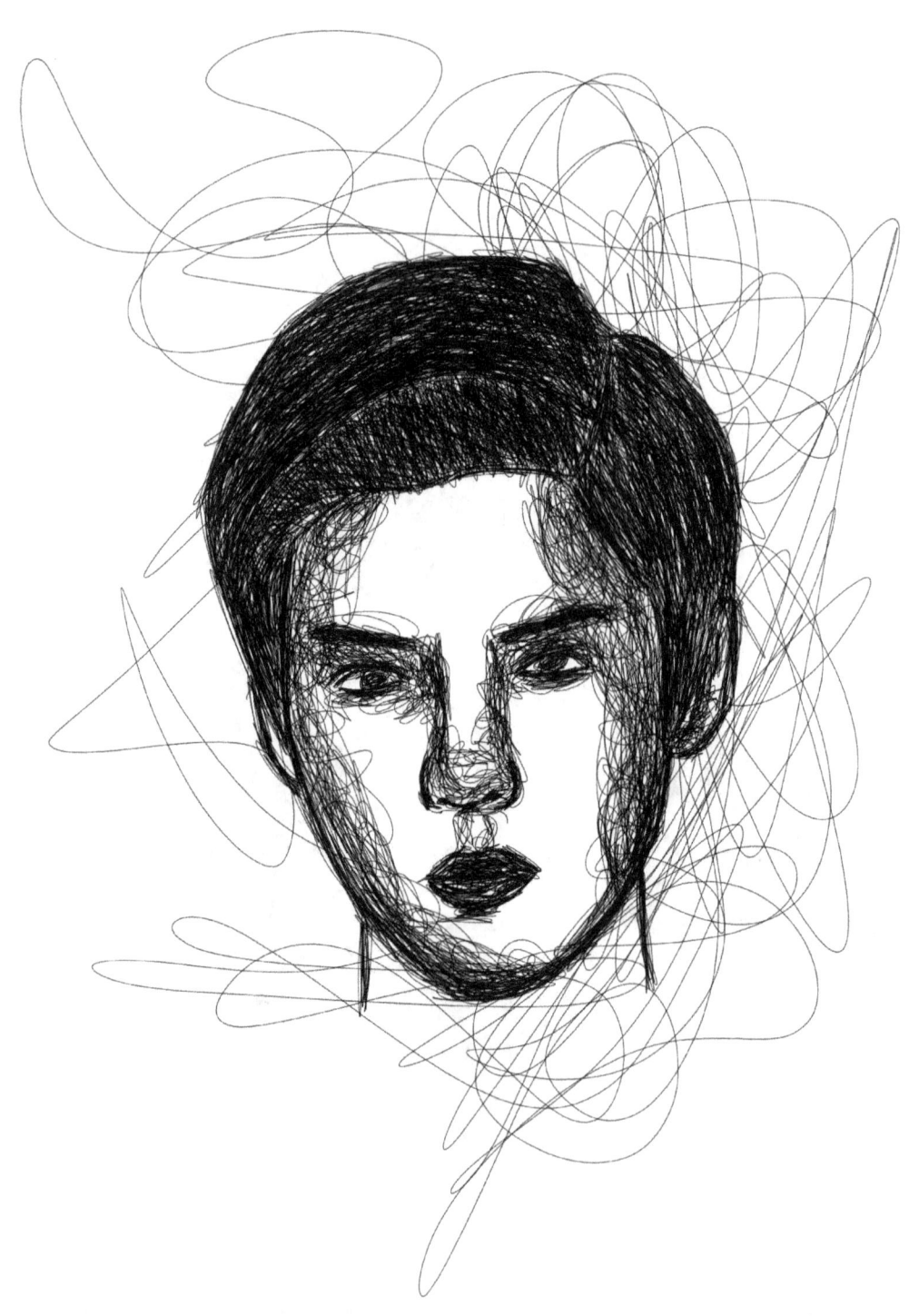

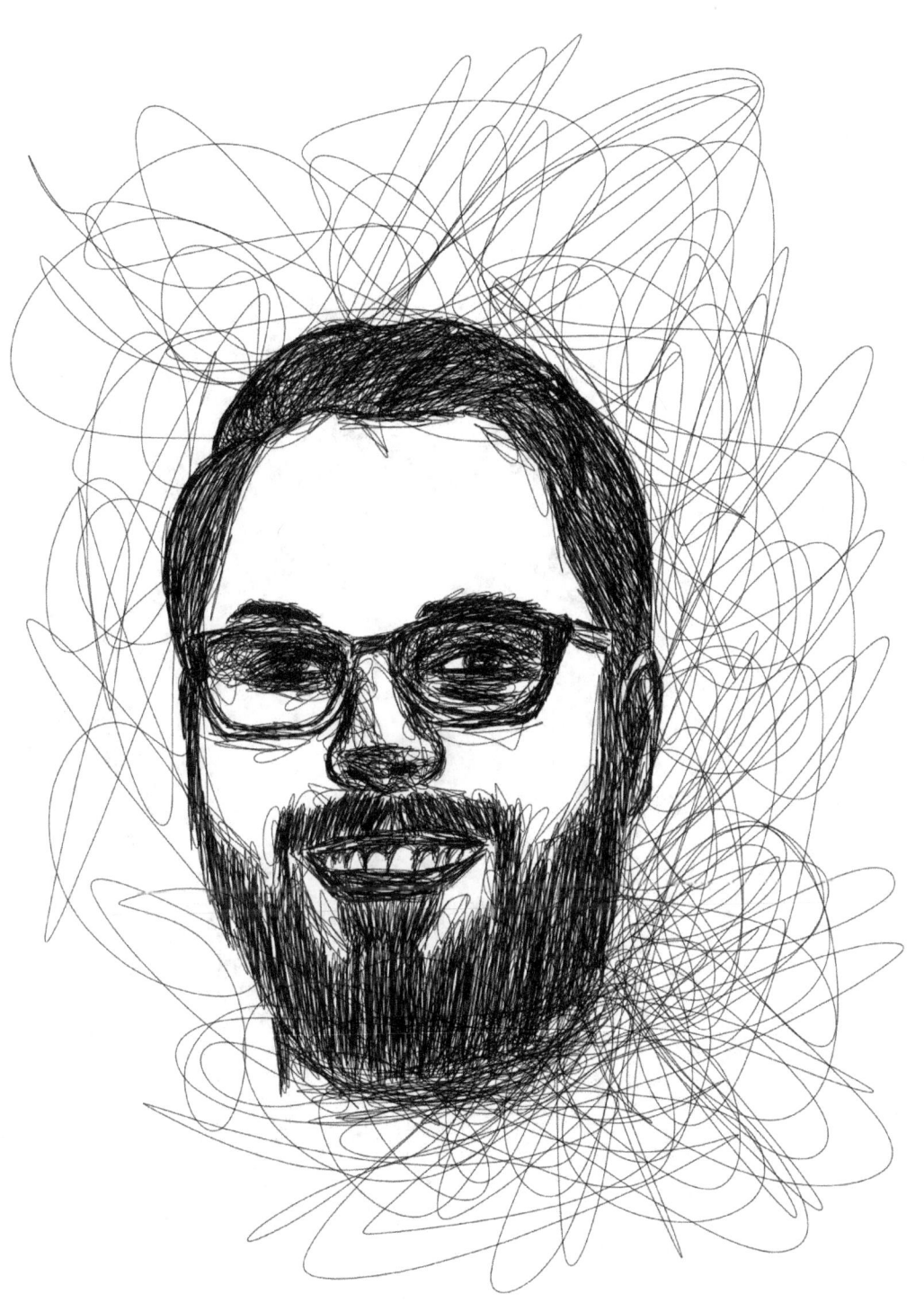

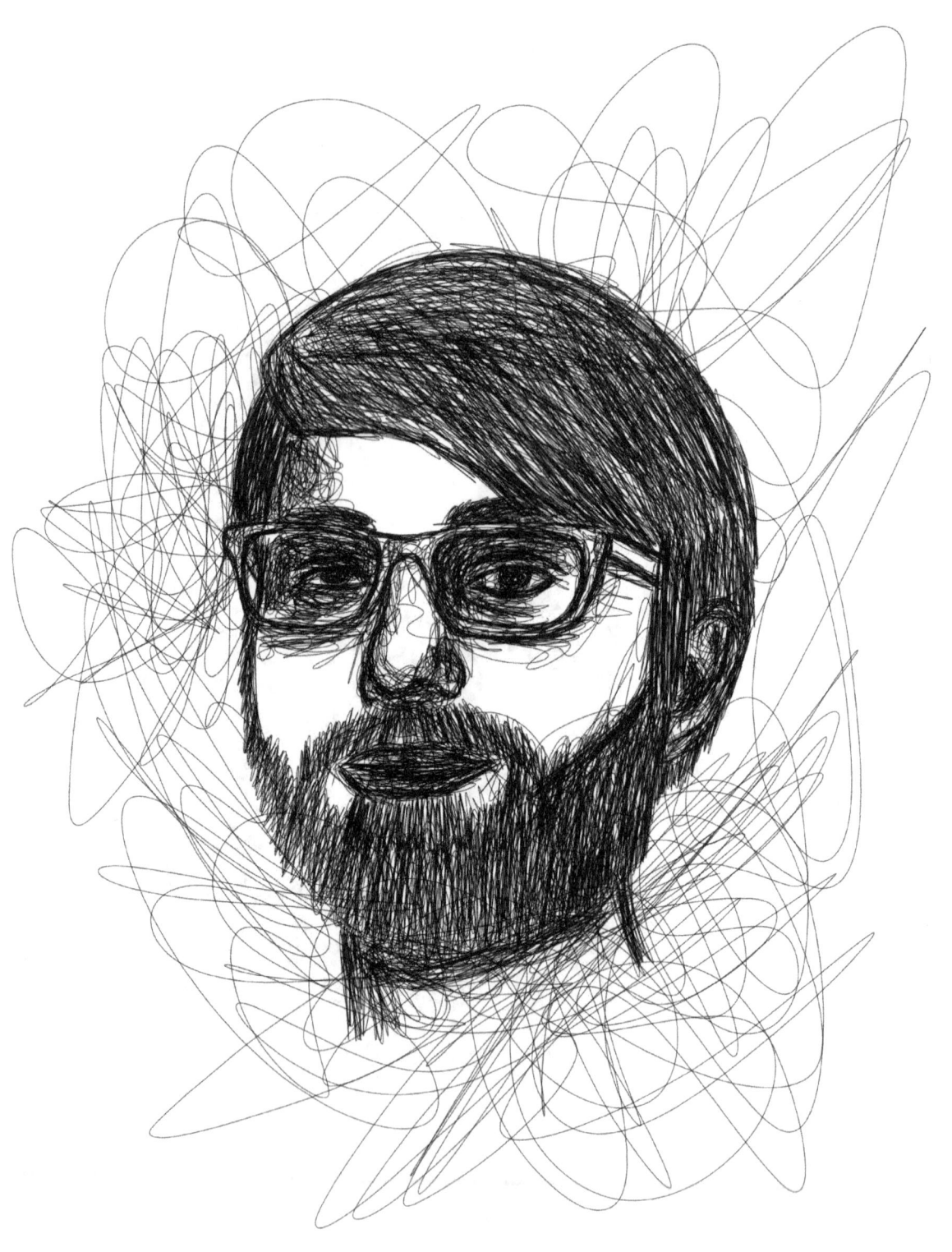

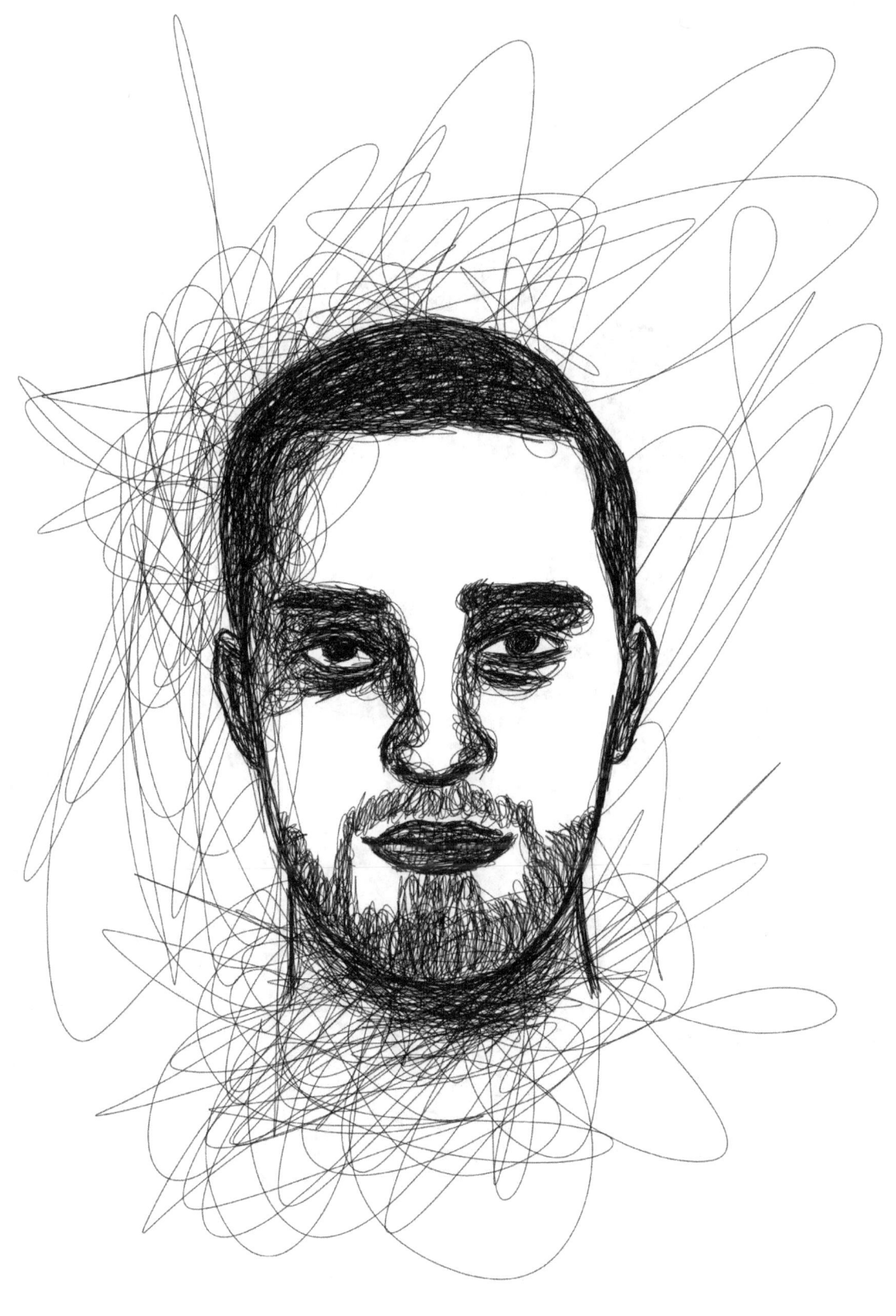

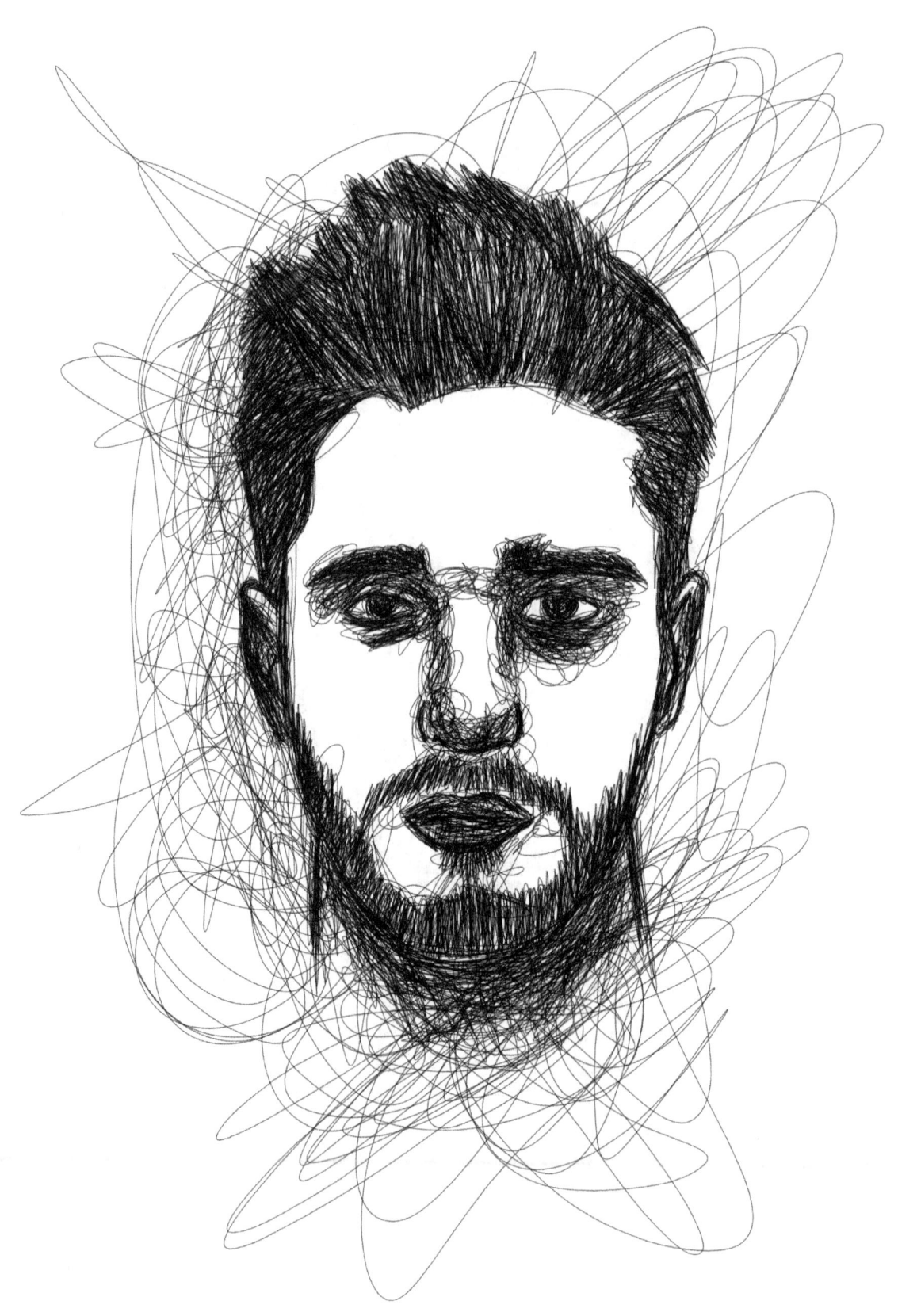

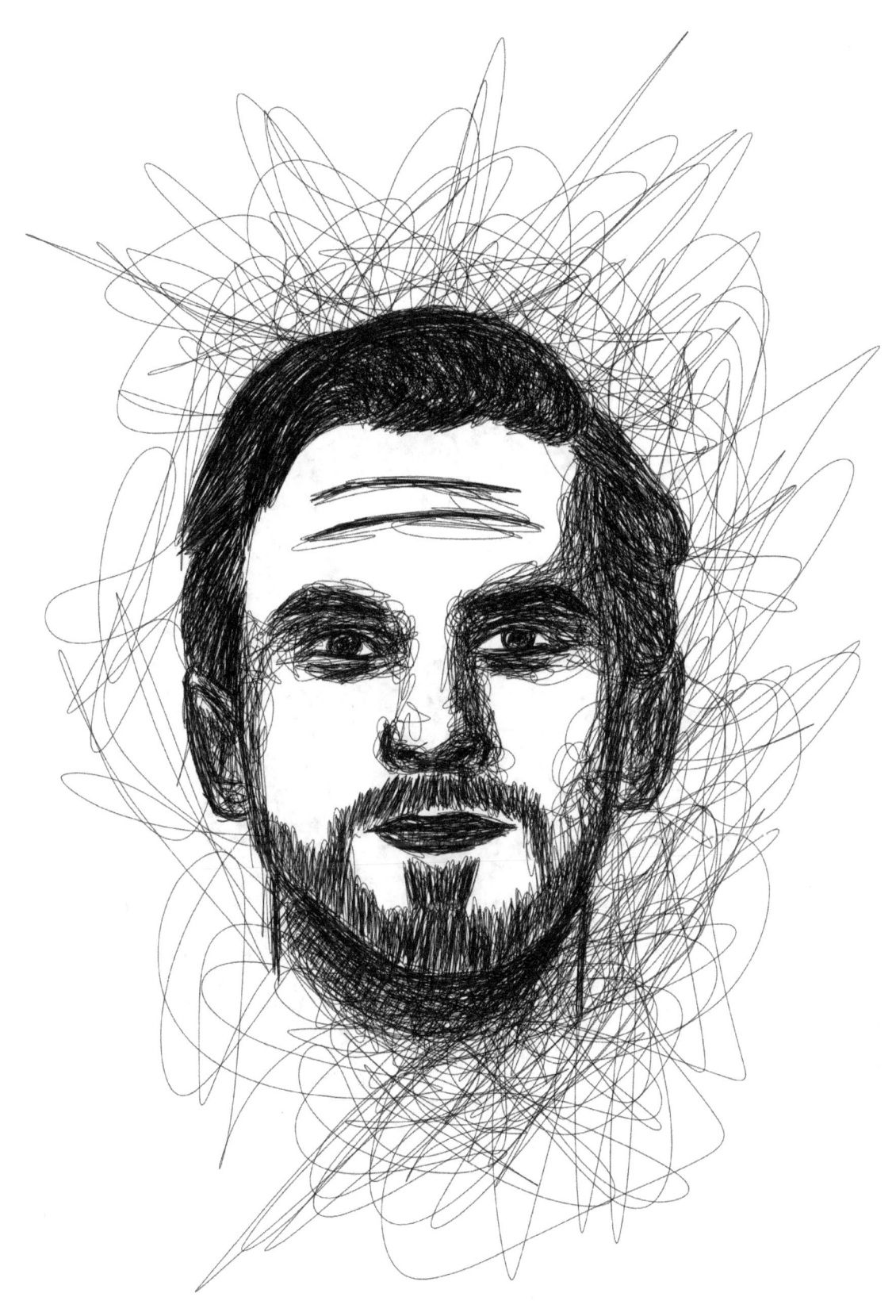

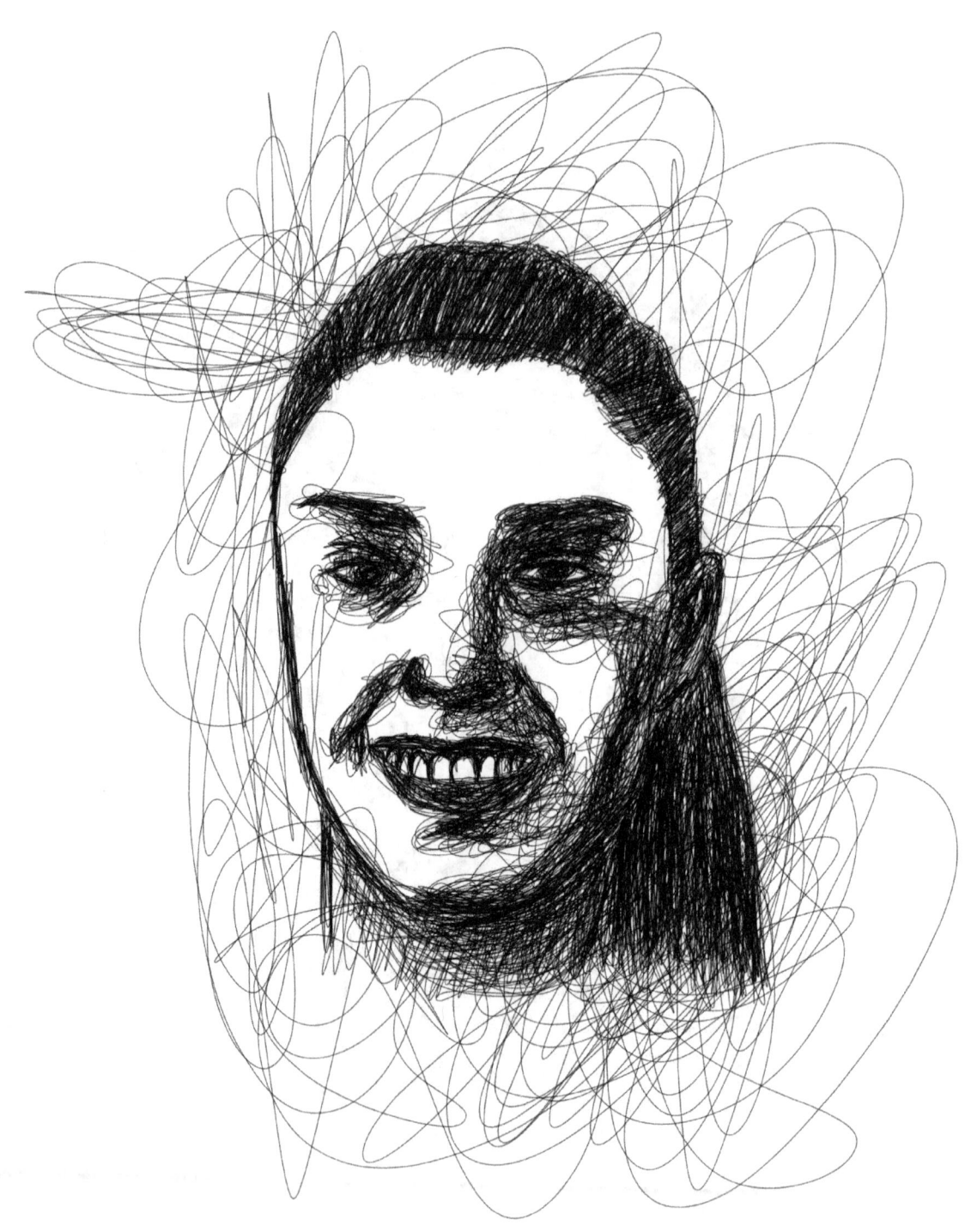

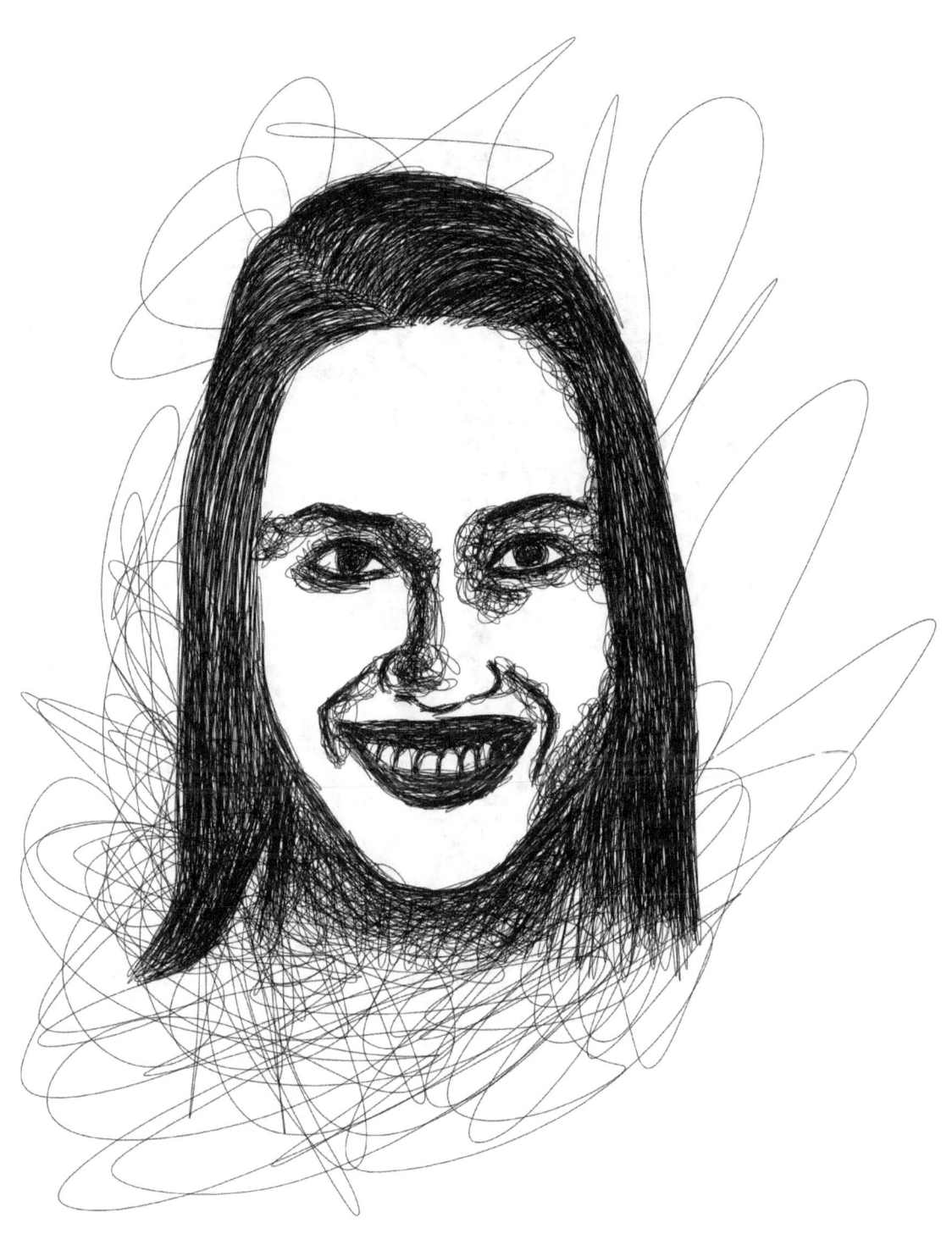

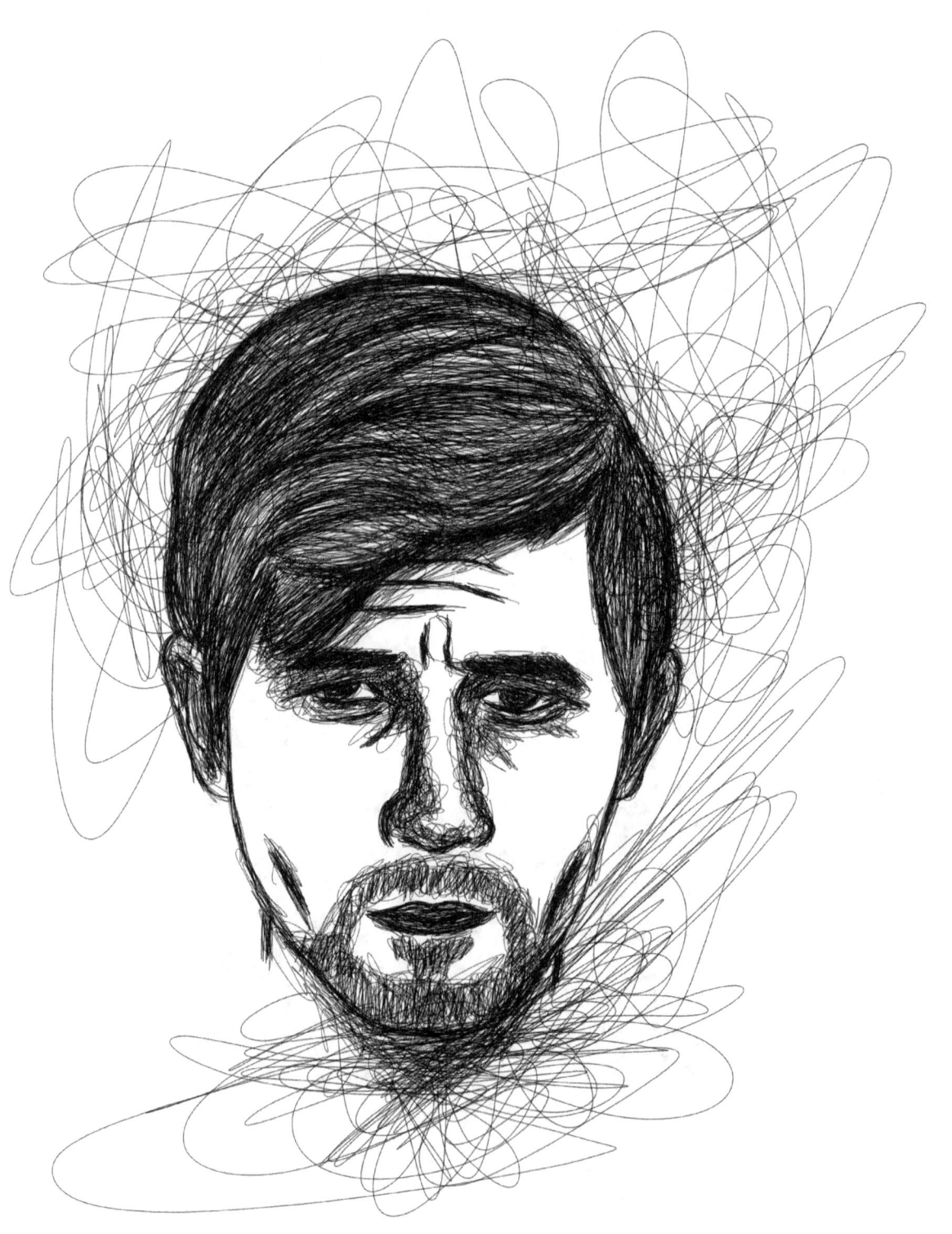

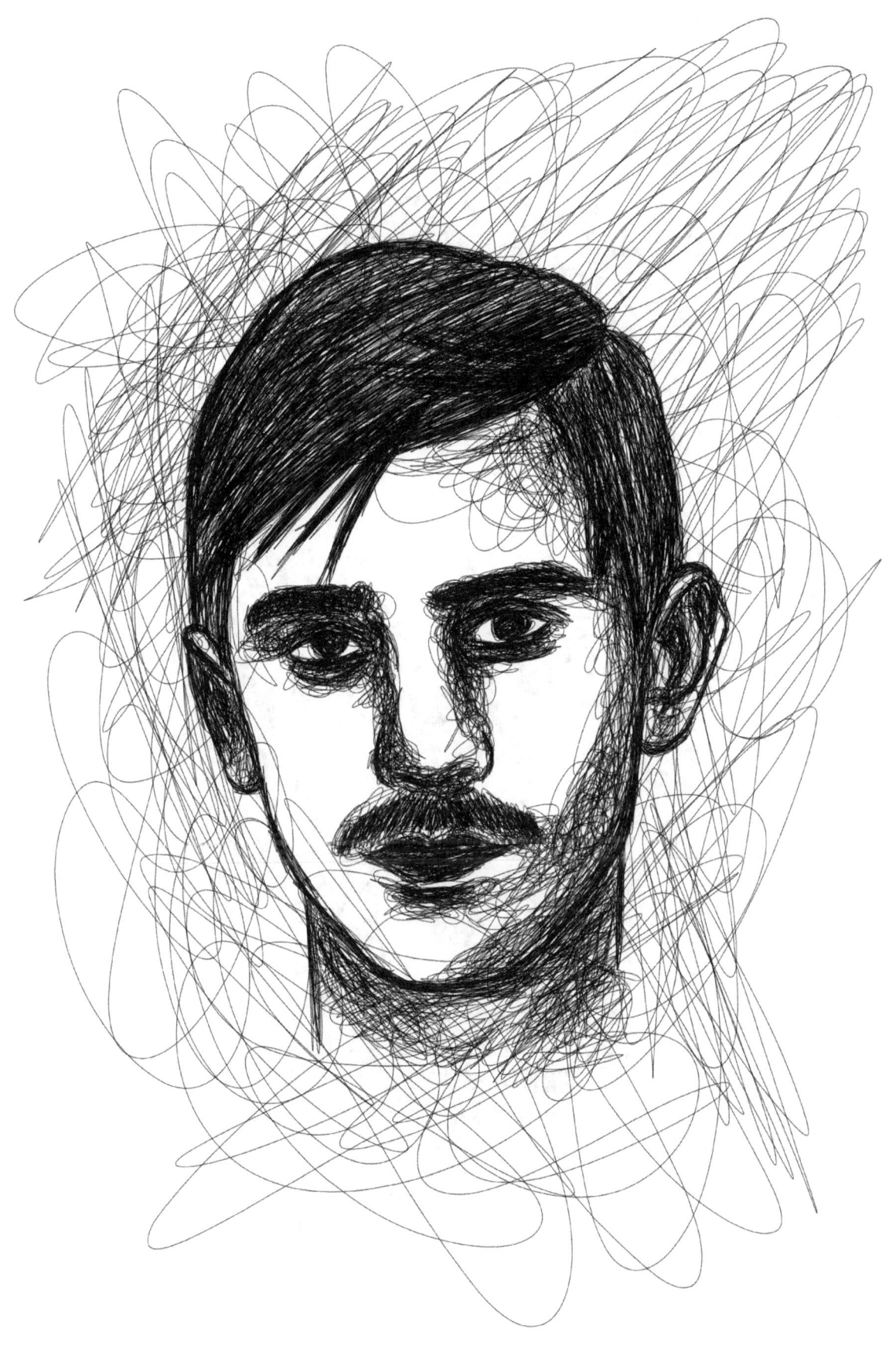

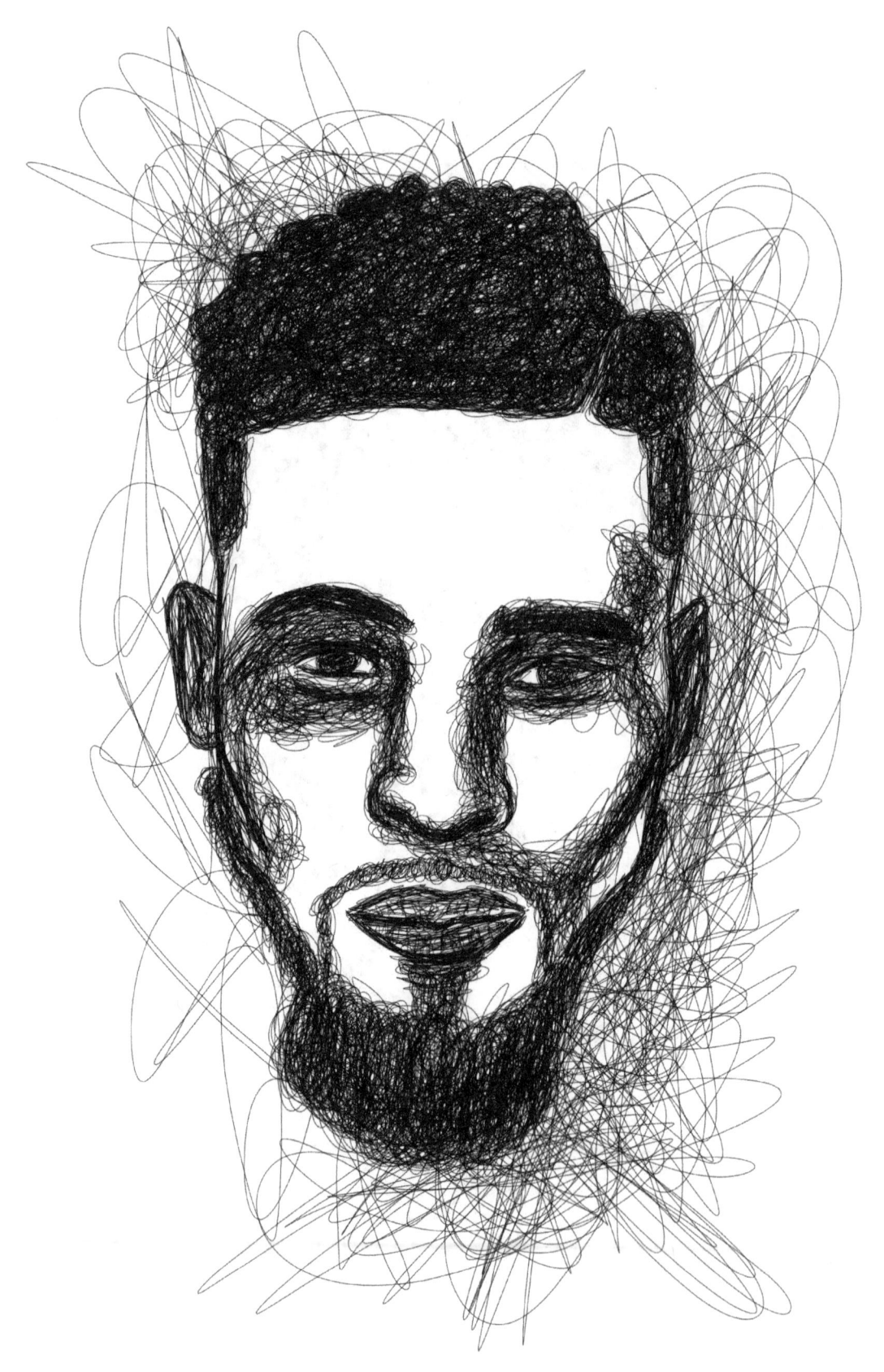

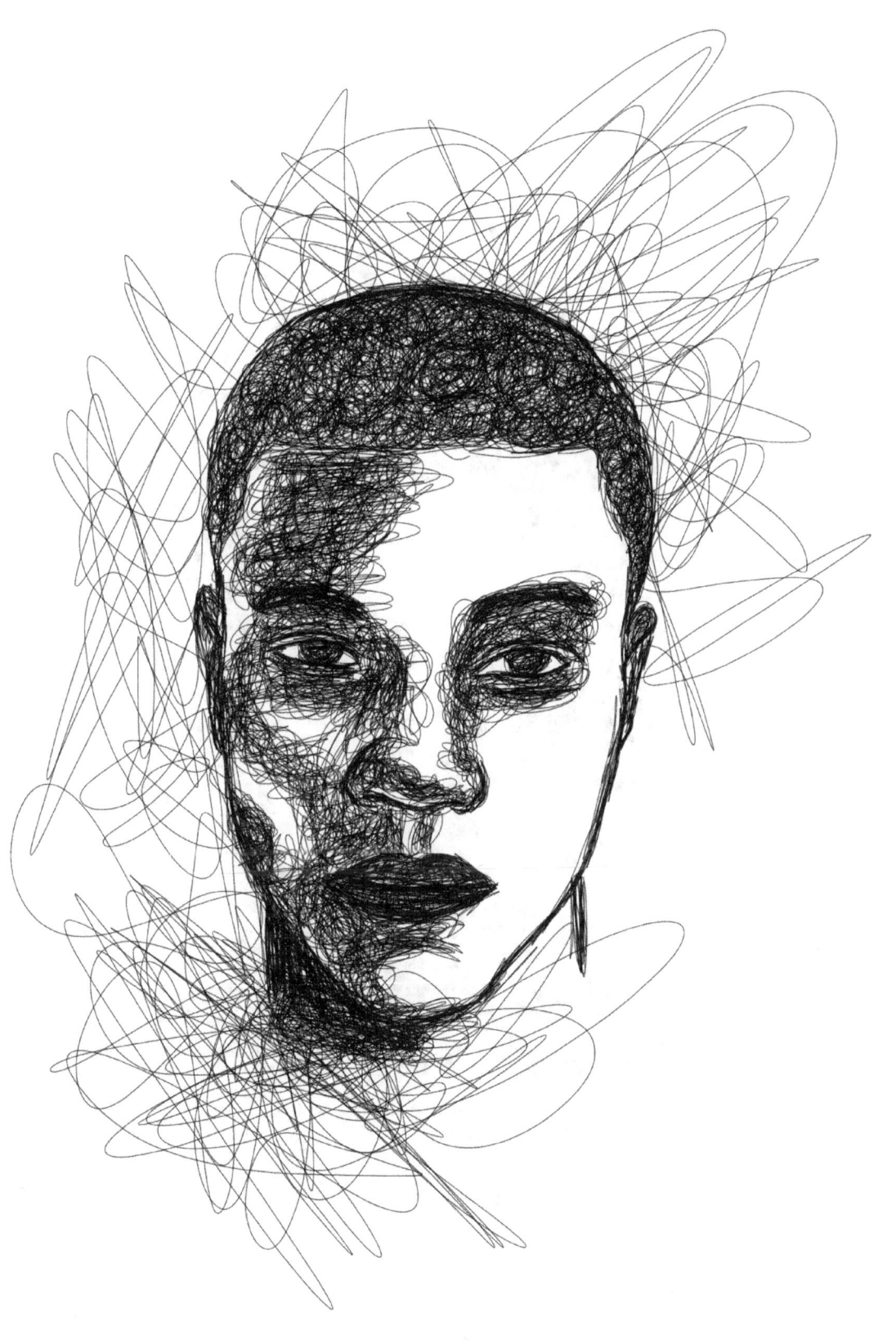

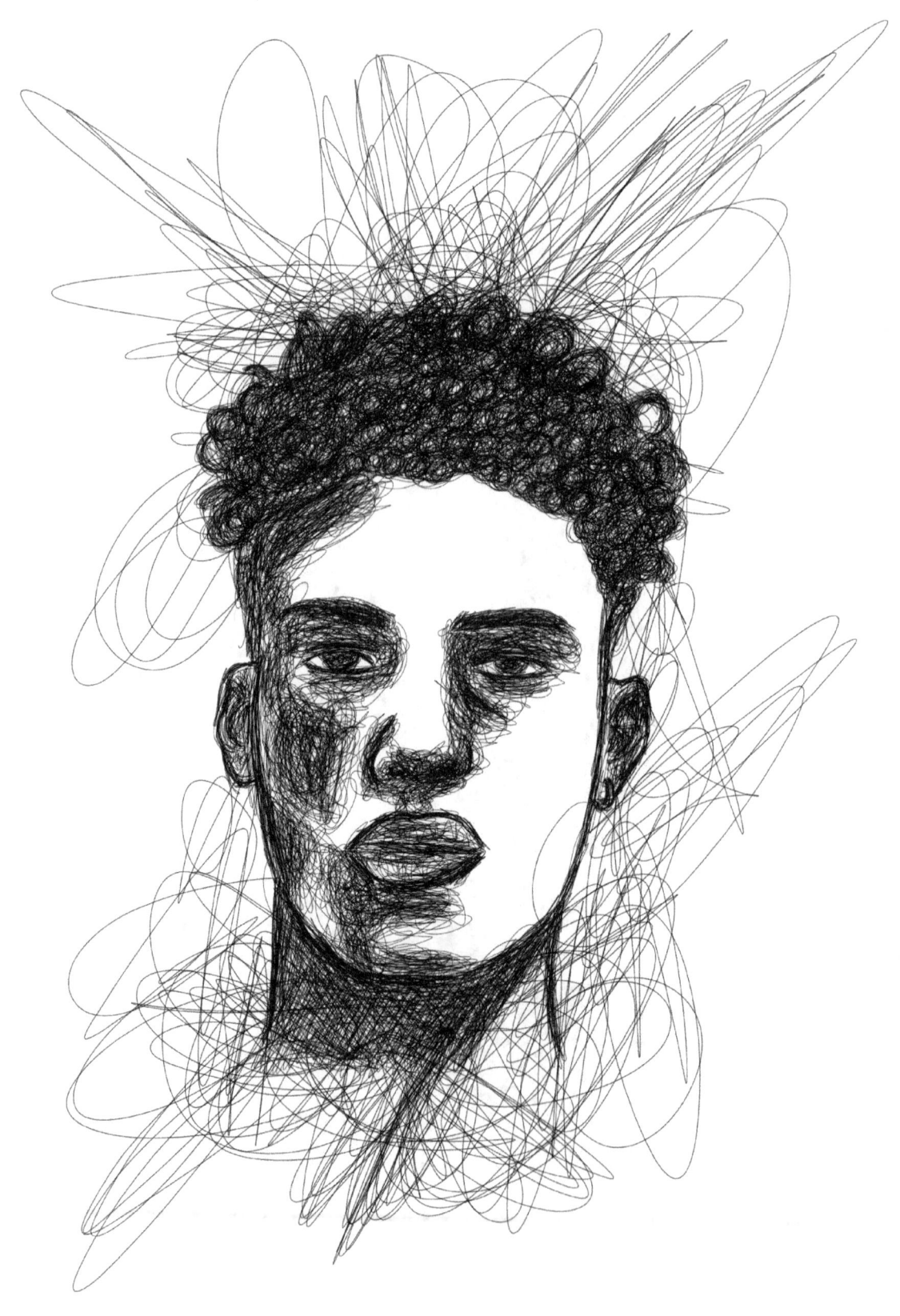

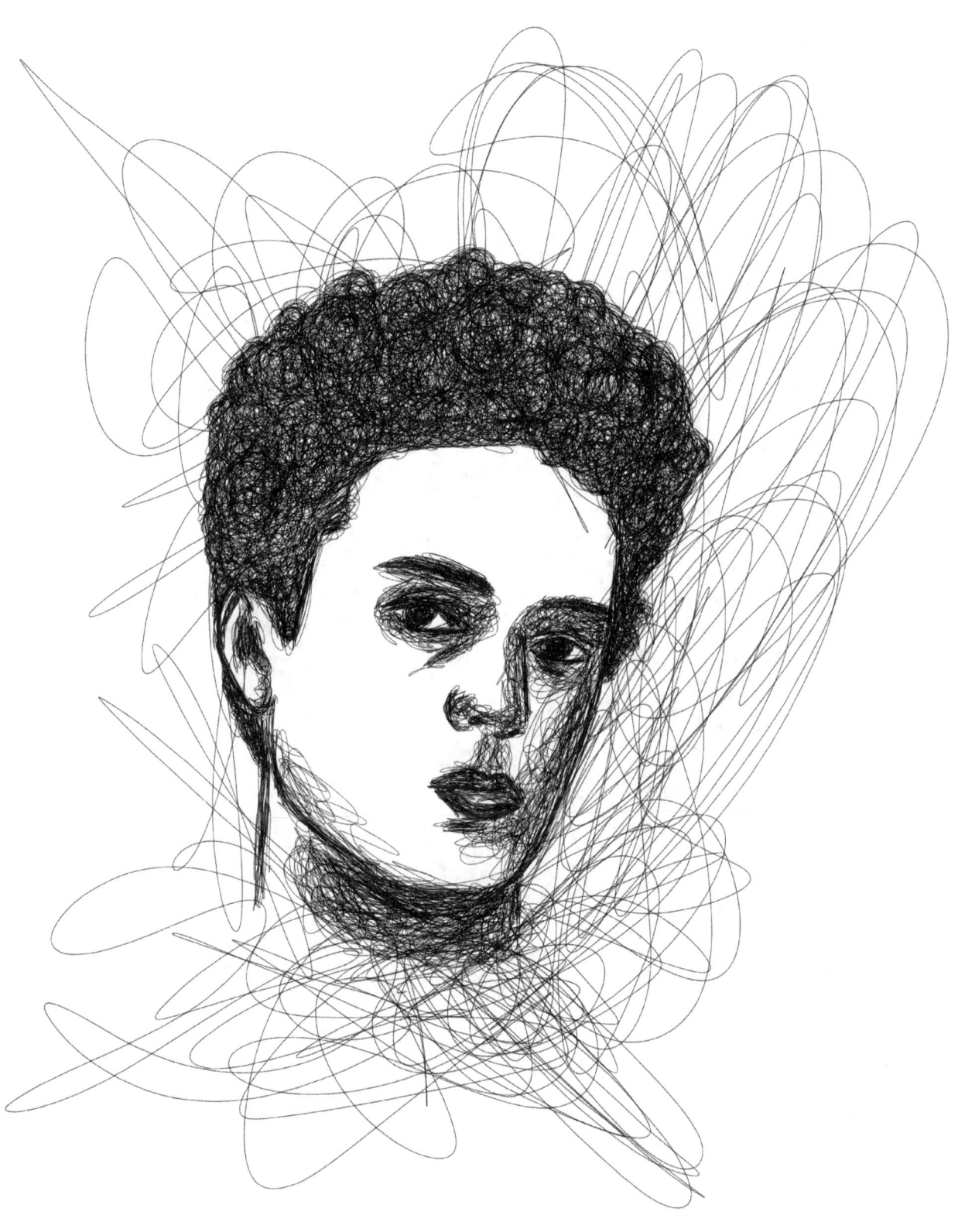

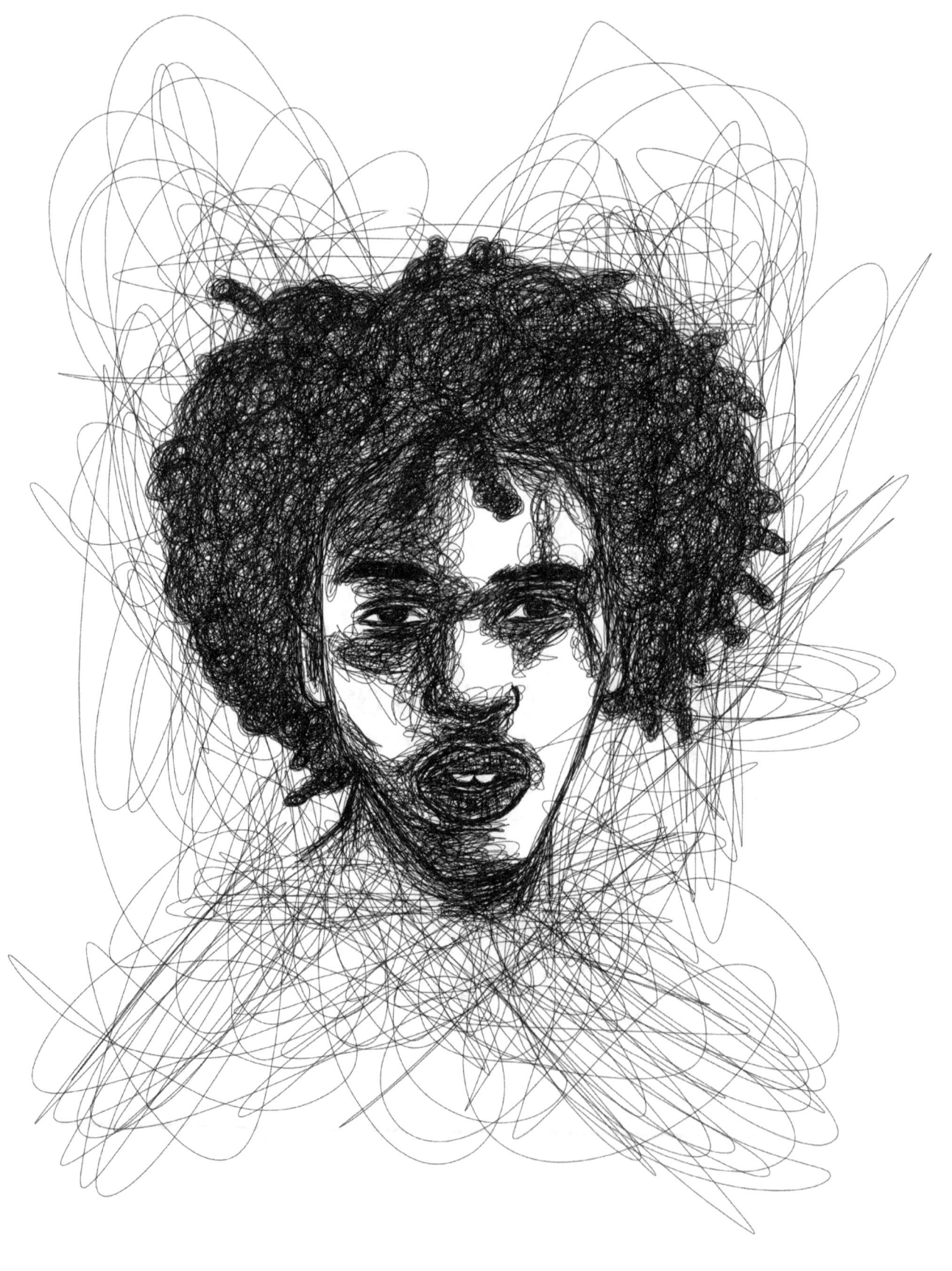

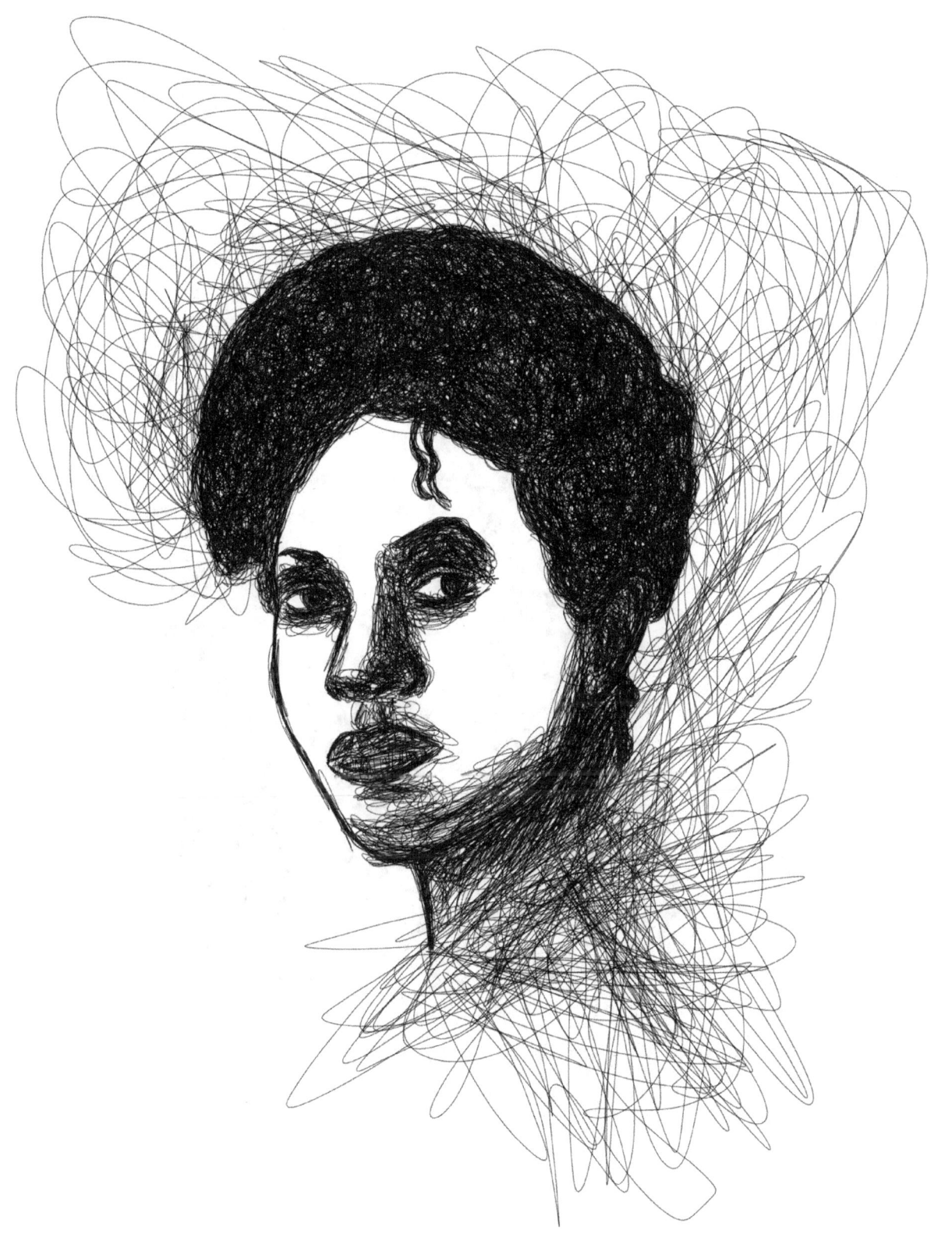

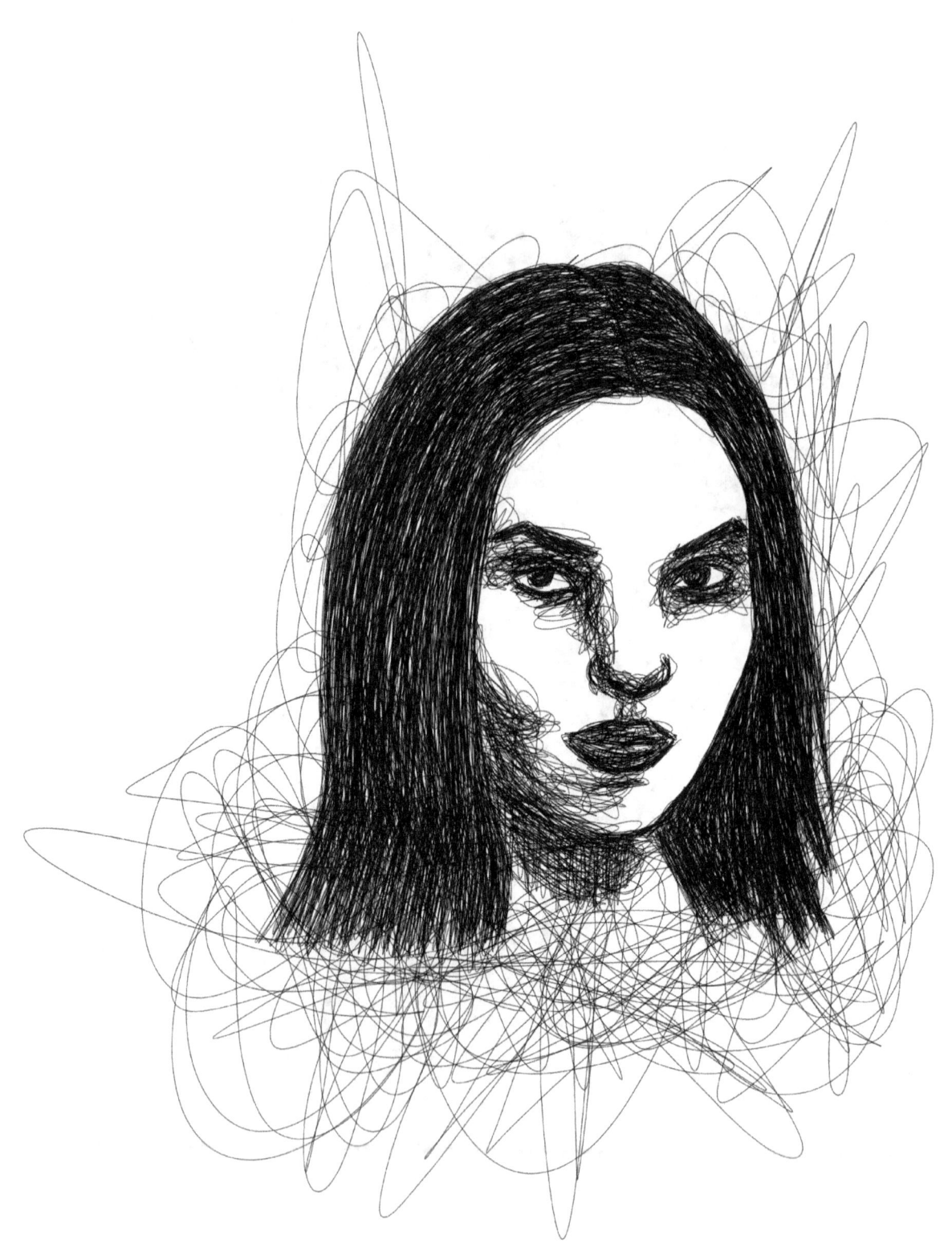

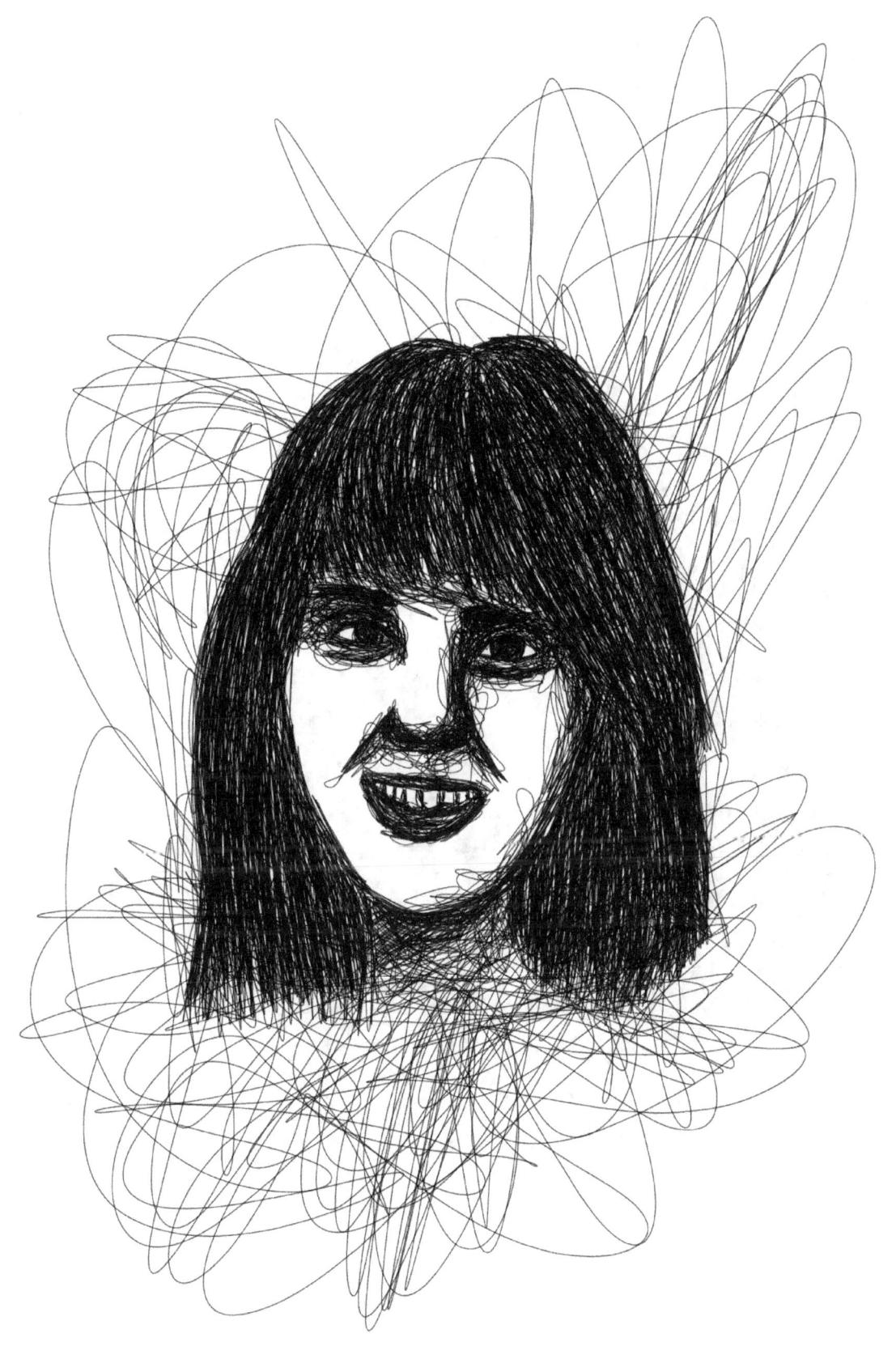

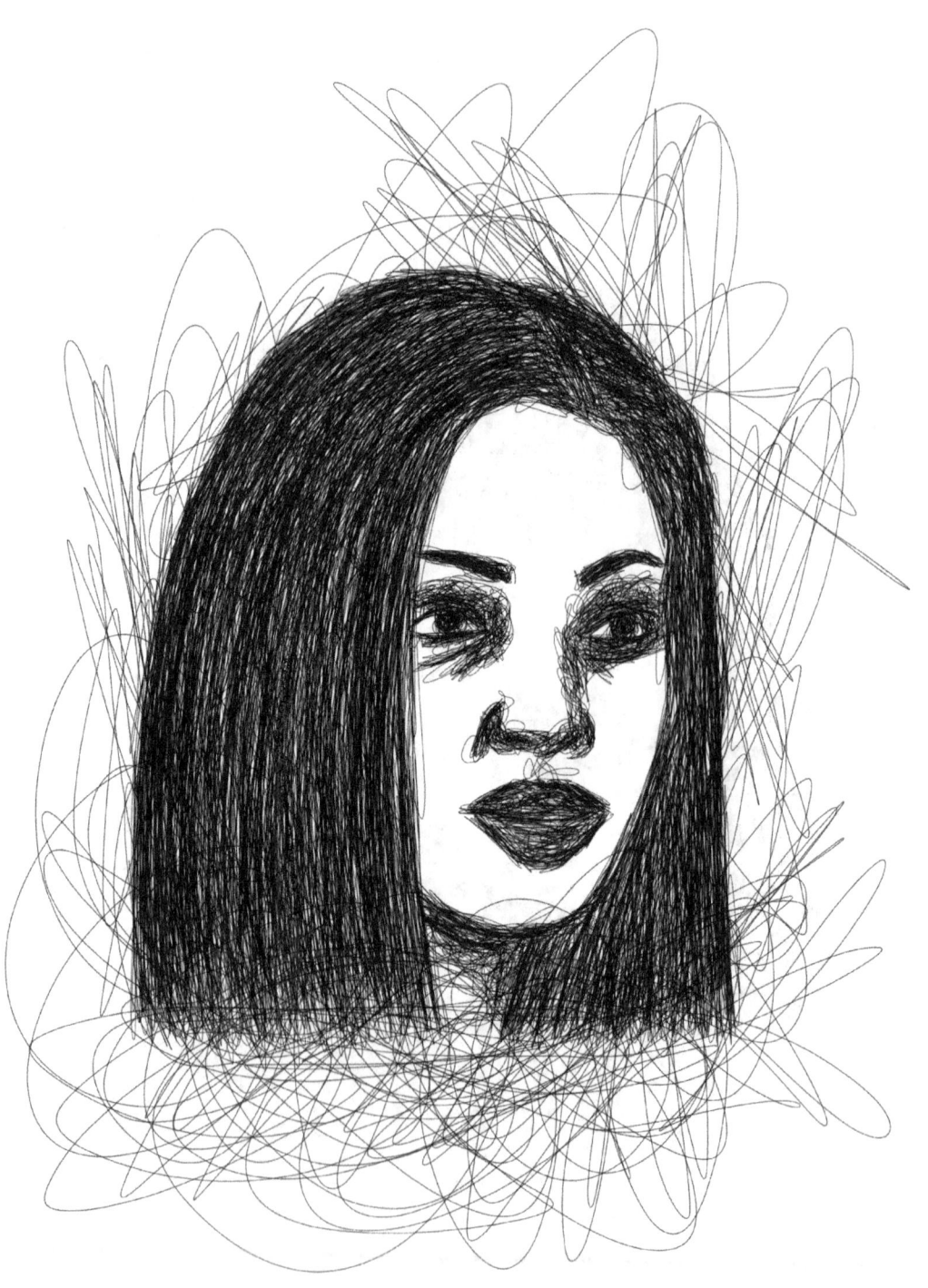

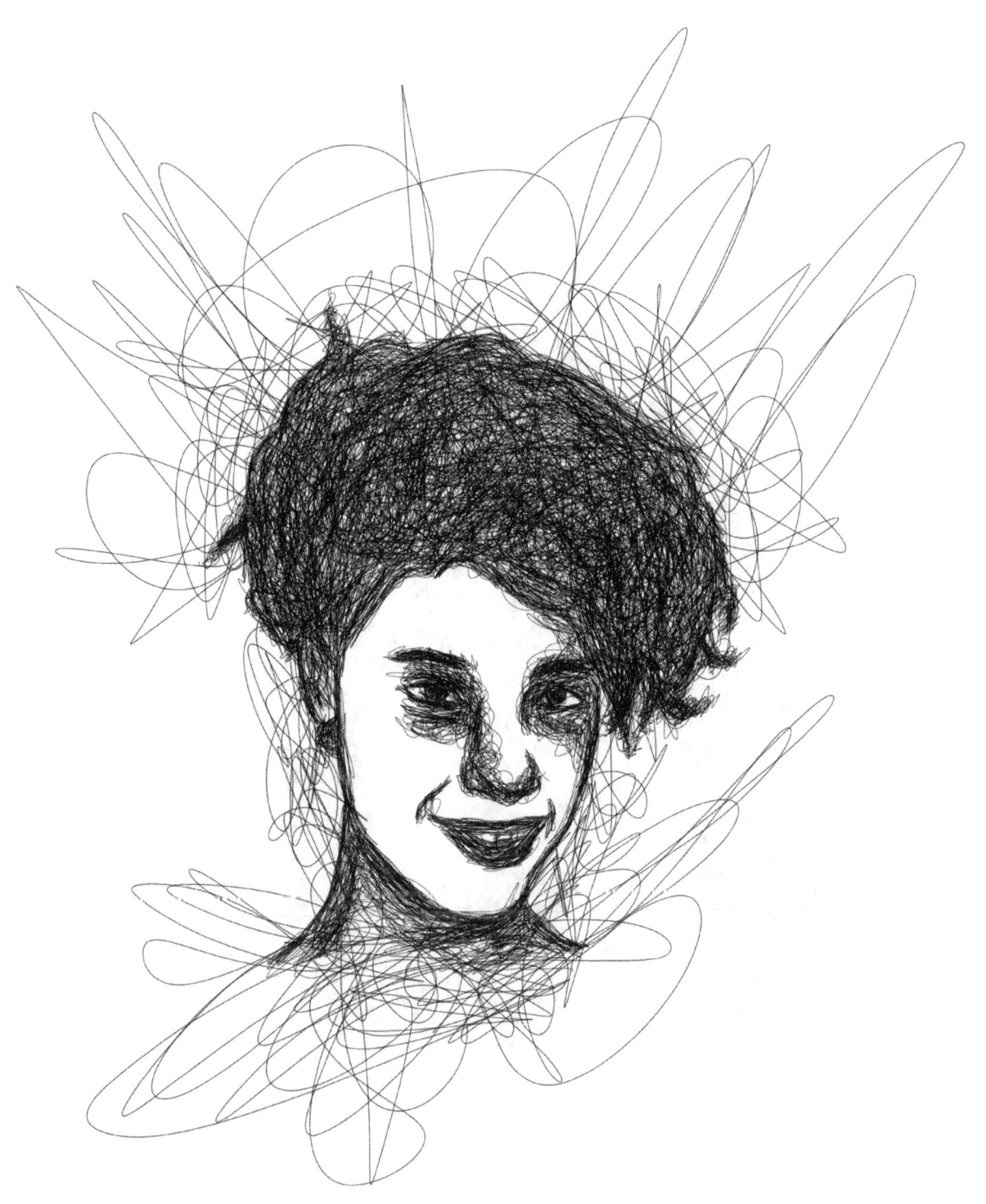

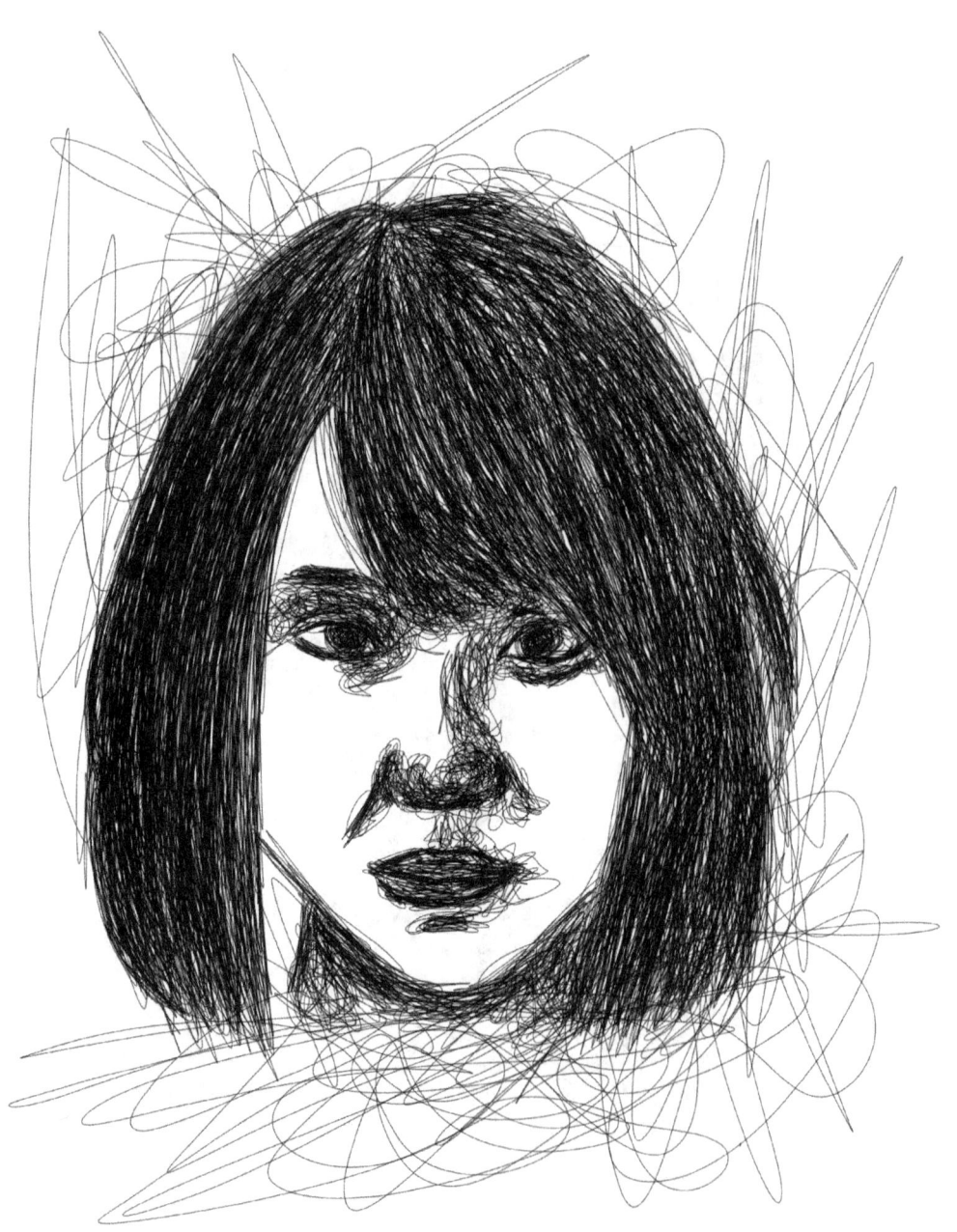

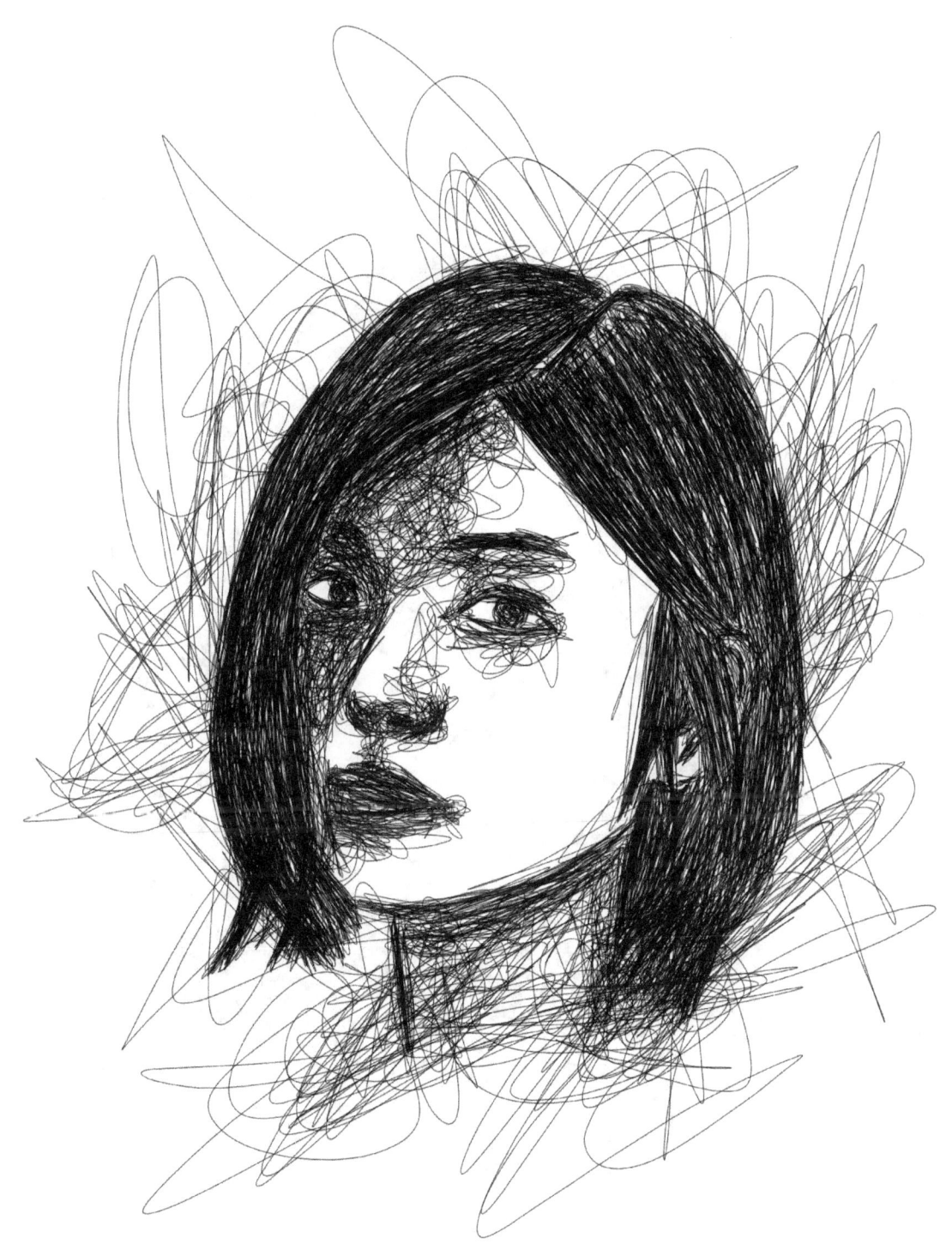

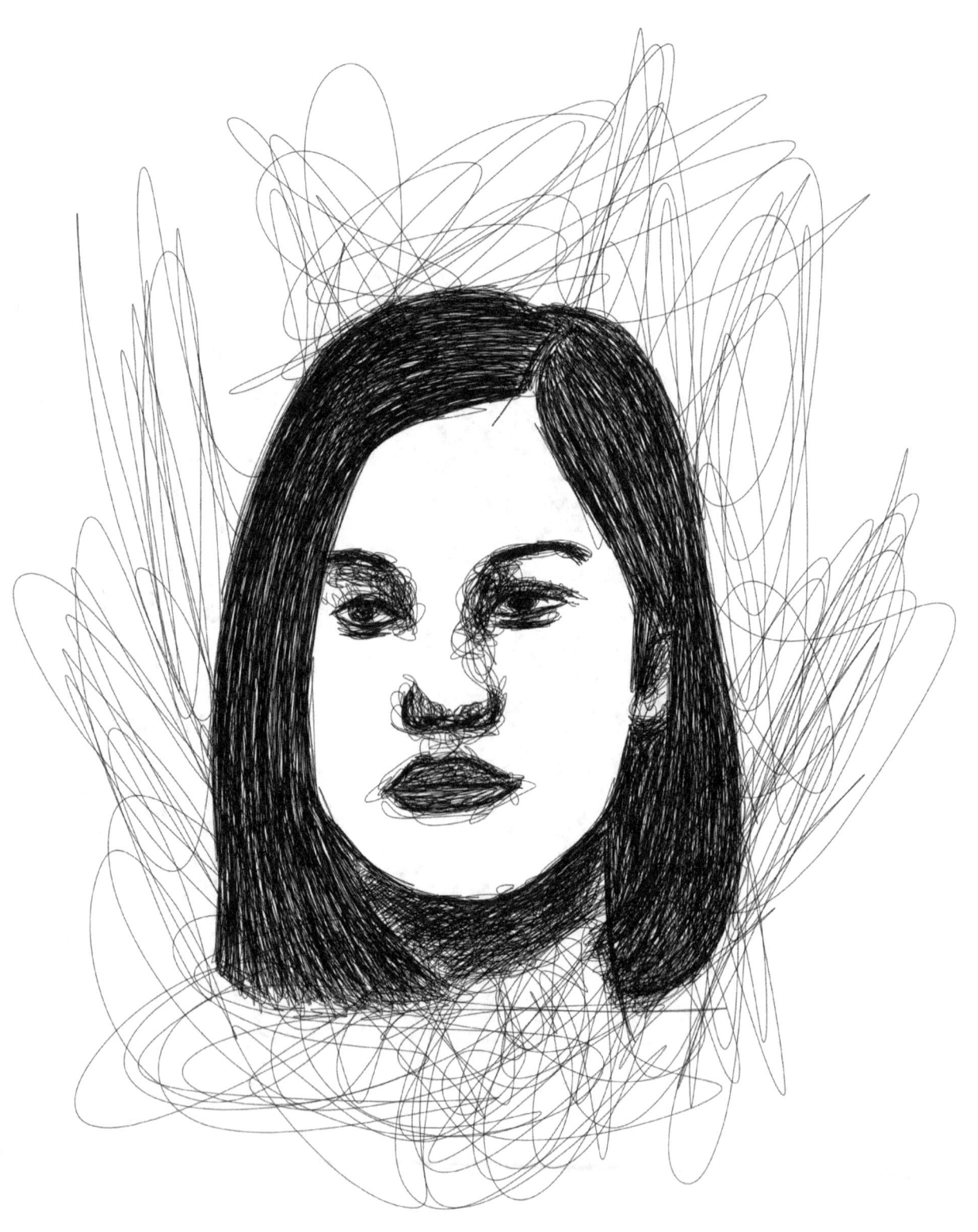

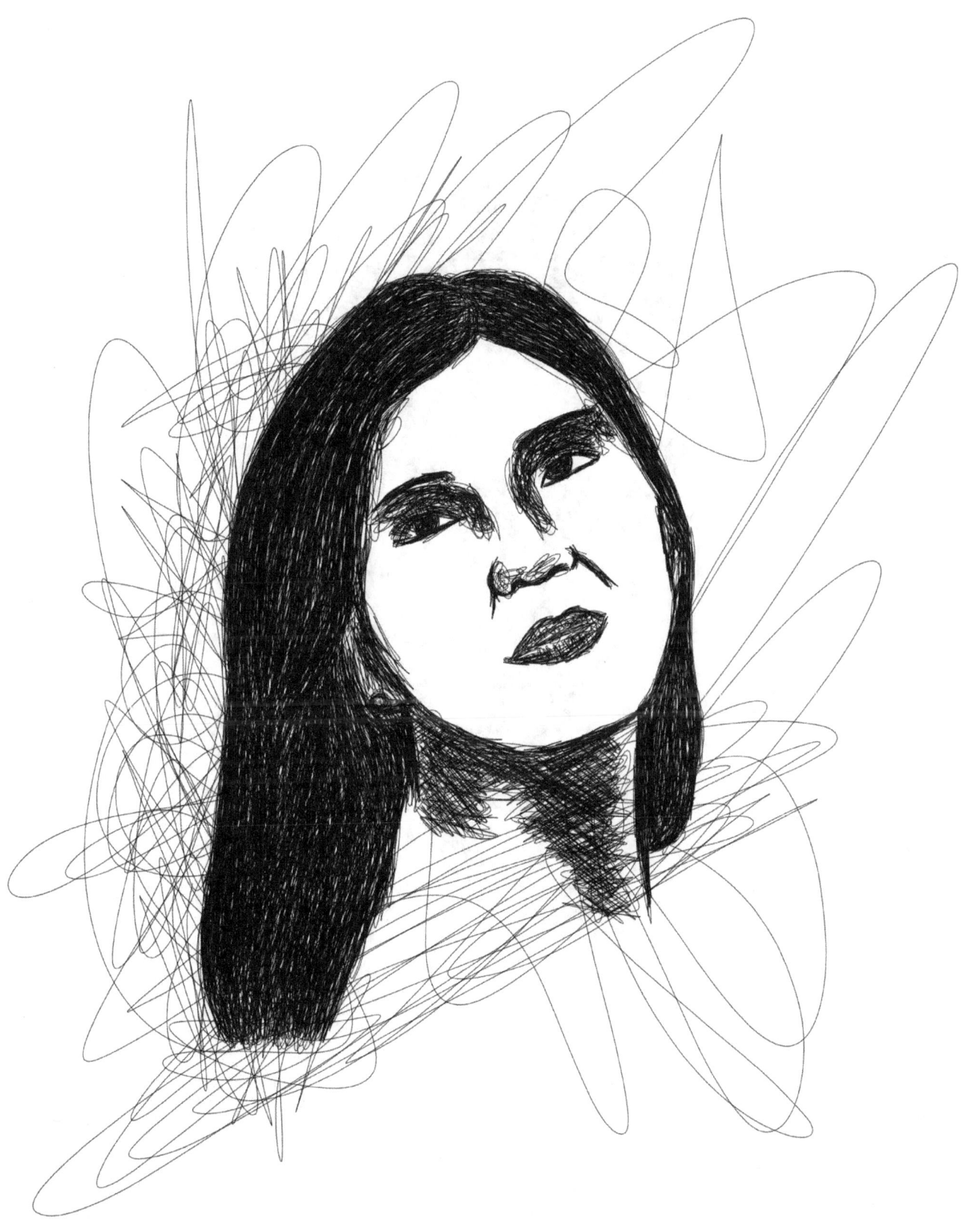

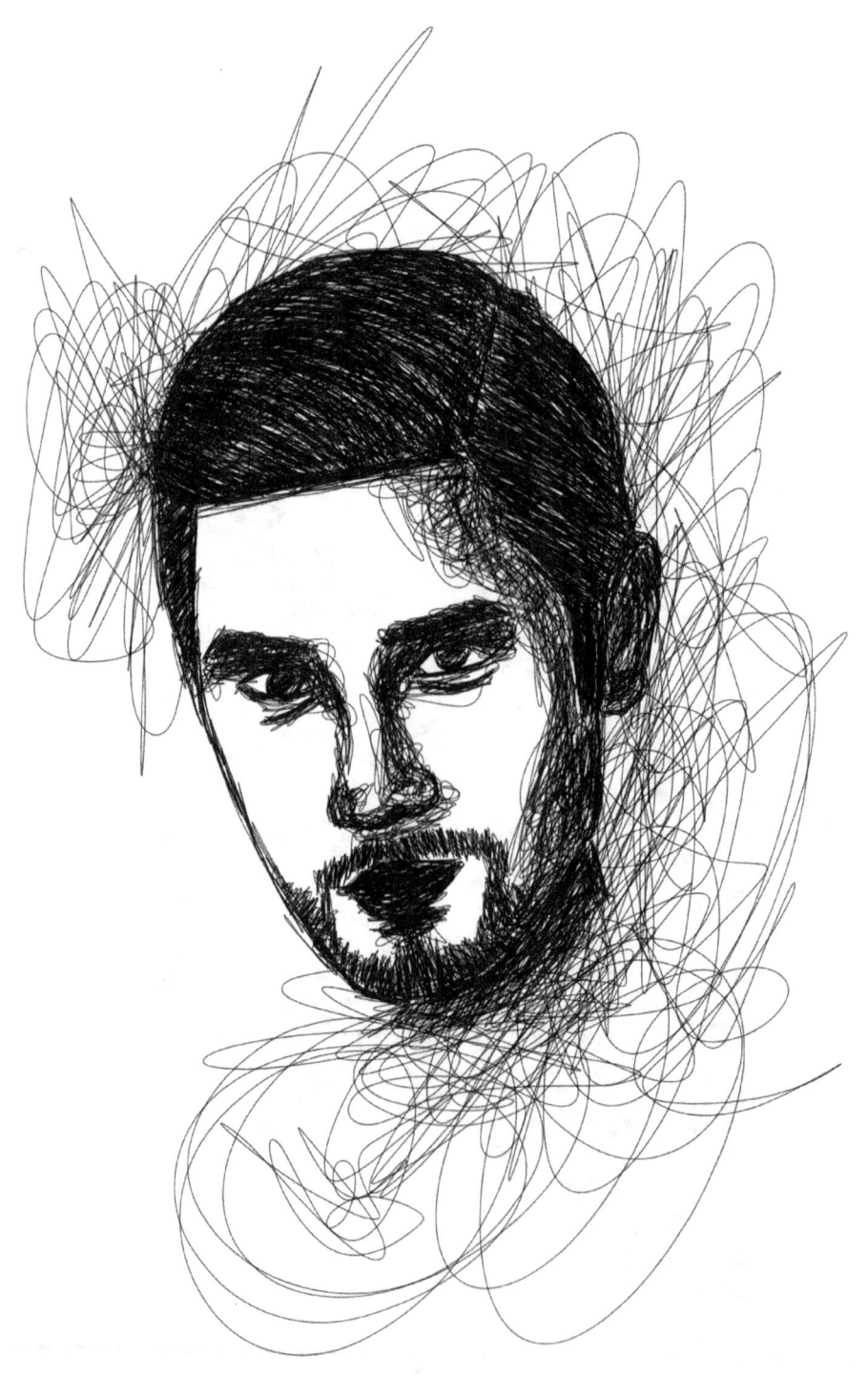

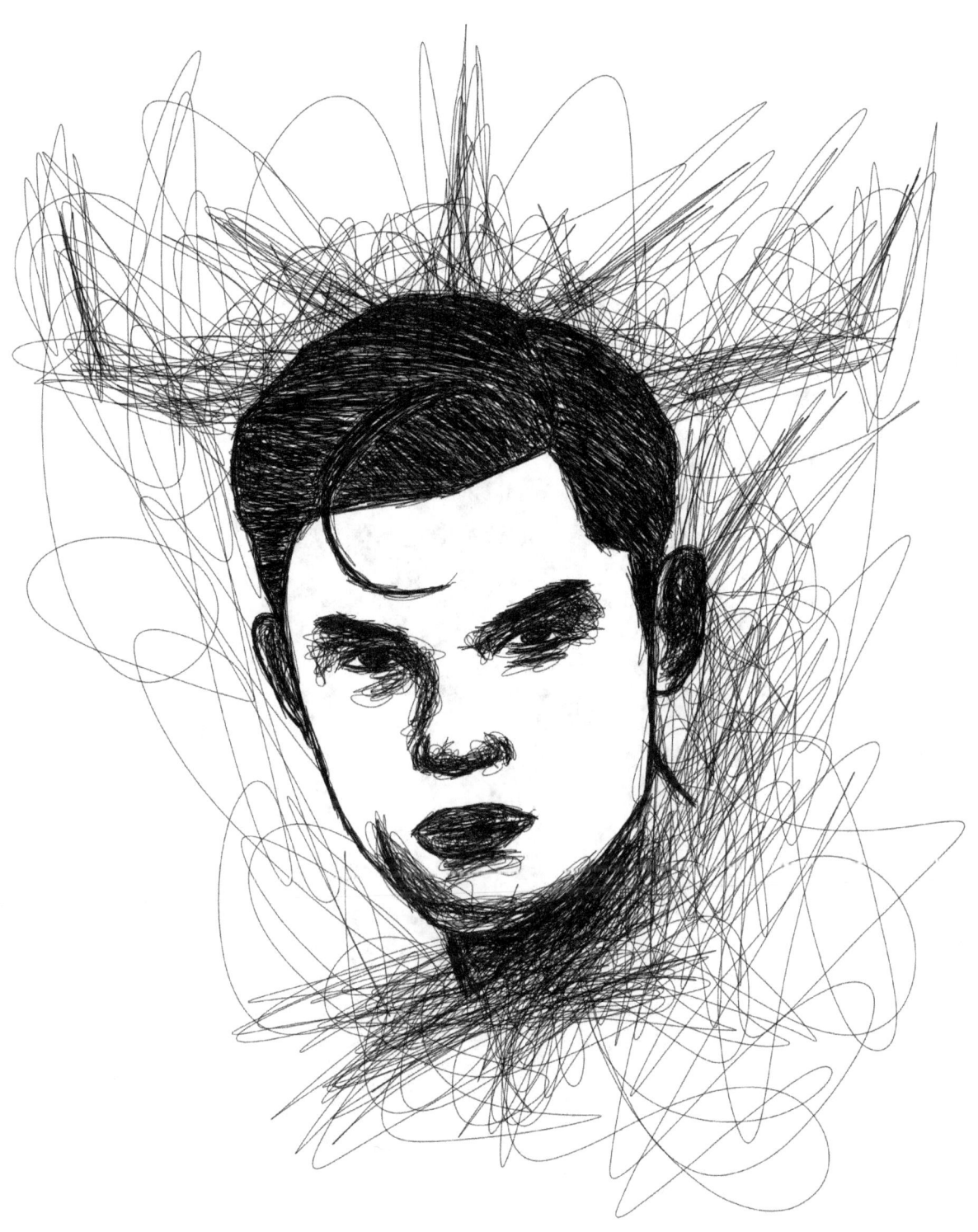

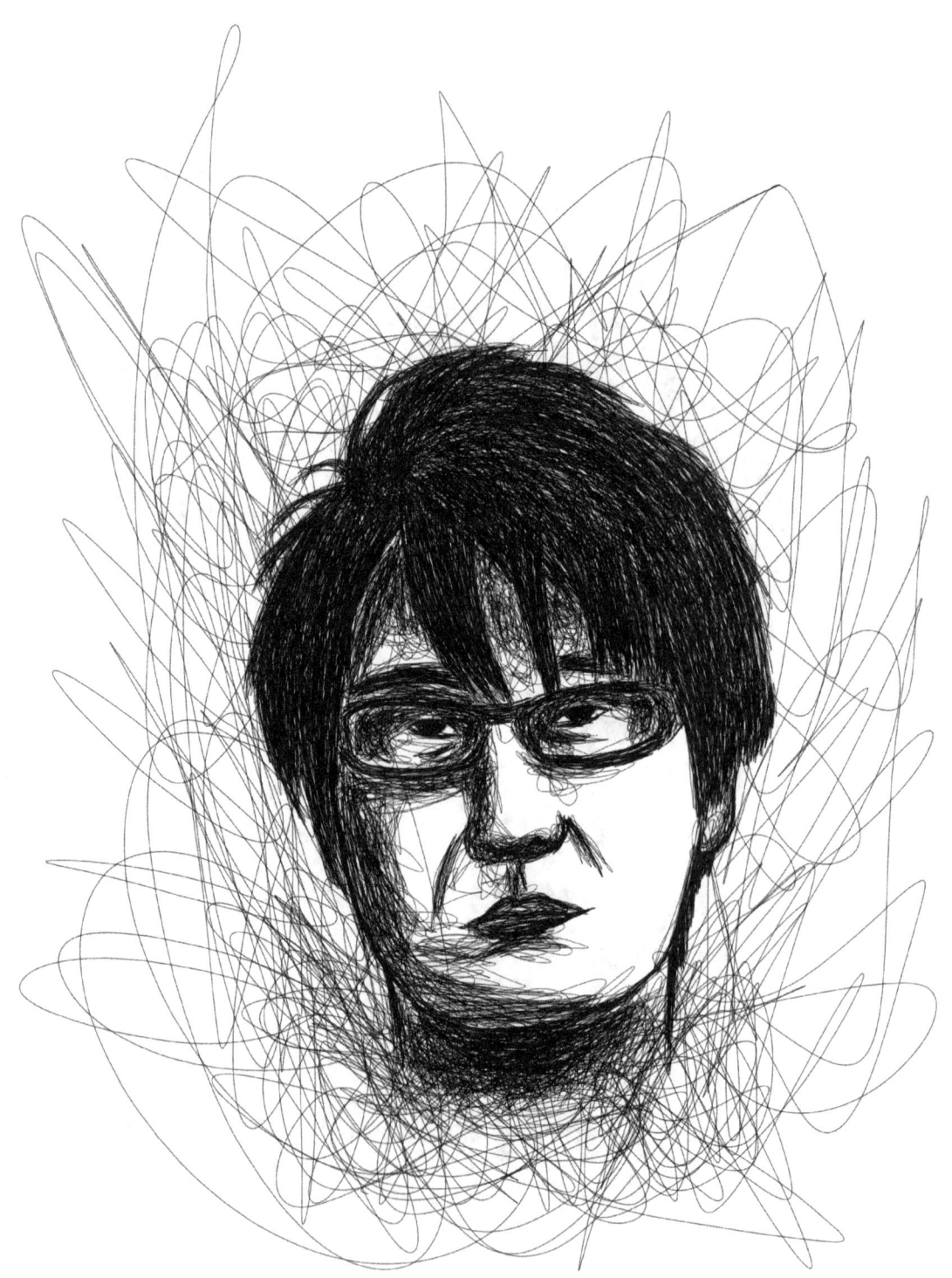

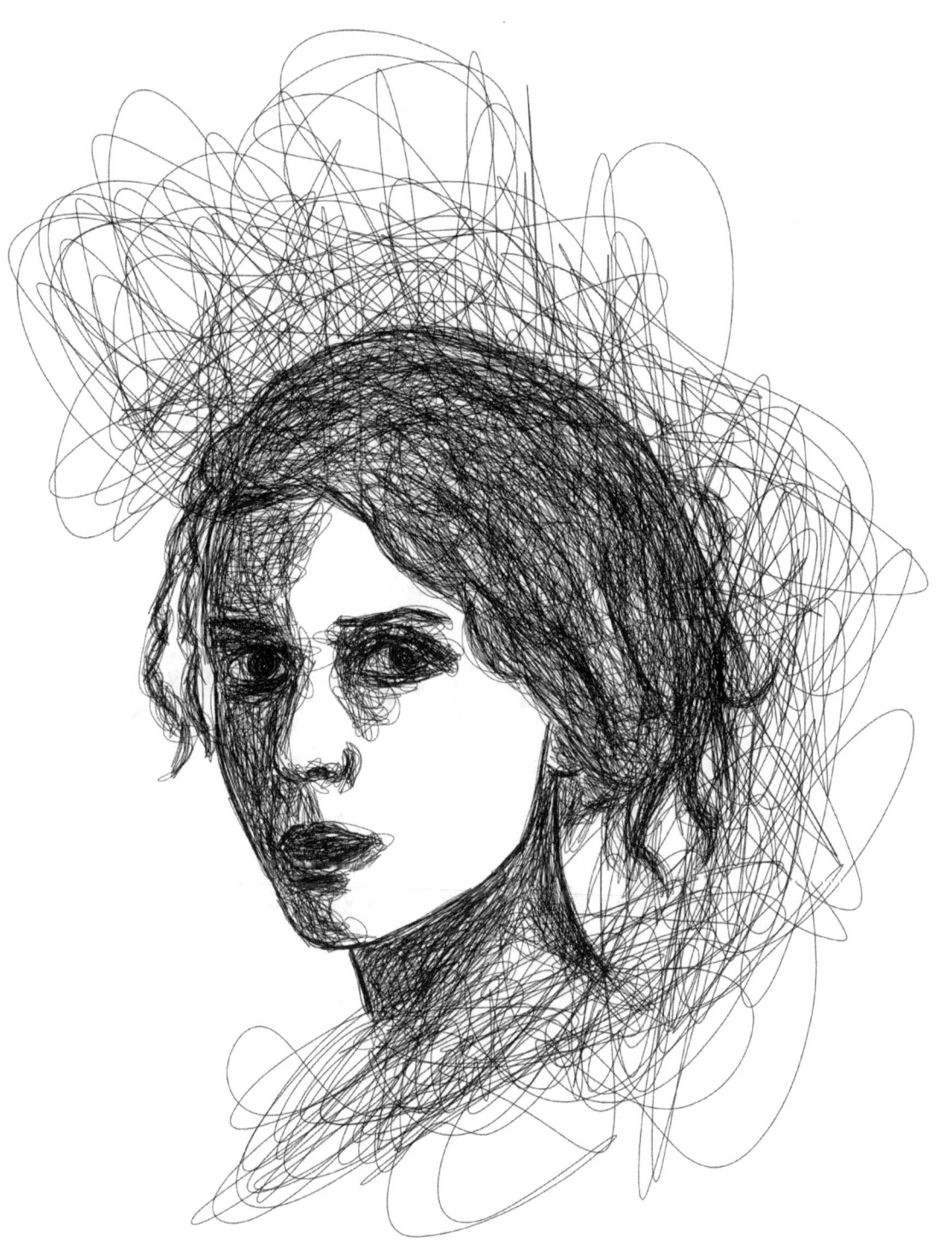

ABOUT THE AUTHOR

Slow decay and eventual death.

www.ingramcontent.com/pod-product-compliance
Lightning Source LLC
Chambersburg PA
CBHW062231220526
45471CB00009B/3431